FOR
THE BOOK

"Gary Hart's intelligence is mixed with a gift for practicality and simplicity, and he is one of the most prescient and important voices in public life. This book is another incredible example of the power of Gary's voice and how urgent the situation is right now for things to change. This essay examines how the restoration of the republic is the best way to save American democracy. Having read it, as well as having the privilege of sitting on his deck in Colorado talking with him, I am sure you will agree with me as to how lucky this country is to have Gary Hart's voice, one that has been in service to this republic for most of his life. . . . Senator Hart's voice can heal the country and chart a real course toward equality, freedom, and hope for all."

—Hugh Jackman

"Gary Hart has always been a thoughtful man and he has written a thoughtful book; a warning, that teeters at times on the brink of despair. If the United States continues down the path that Donald Trump forged, Hart fears, then we are well on our way to losing our republic. If that prospect alarms you, read this slim volume . . . and buy another copy for a friend."

—Ted Koppel

"Gary Hart's eloquent call to action could not be more timely. This important new book makes a compelling argument that saving American democracy demands restoring our republic and reinvigorating the civic virtues that sustain it. At this moment of maximum peril, every patriotic American should read what Senator Hart has to say."

—Laurence H. Tribe,
University Professor of
Constitutional Law Emeritus,
Harvard University

"In this clearly and vigorously written book, former Senator Gary Hart invokes the historic tradition of republicanism, with its prescriptions of popular sovereignty, anti-corruption, and civic virtue, as the best means for saving our beleaguered democracy. His words of wisdom are all the more effective and worth listening to because, as a scholar of history and a participant in government, Hart knows more than most of us about both the outside and the inside of our politics."

—Gordon S. Wood,
Pulitzer Prize winner and
author of *The Radicalism of the American Revolution*

THE AMERICAN REPUBLIC CAN SAVE AMERICAN DEMOCRACY

THE AMERICAN REPUBLIC CAN SAVE AMERICAN DEMOCRACY

GARY HART

Fulcrum Publishing
Wheat Ridge, Colorado

Library of Congress Cataloging-in-Publication Data

Names: Hart, Gary, 1936- author.
Title: The American republic can save American democracy / by Gary
    Hart.
Description: Wheat Ridge, Colorado : Fulcrum Publishing, 2022. |
    Includes
        bibliographical references.
Identifiers: LCCN 2021059401 | ISBN 9781682753392 (paperback)
Subjects: LCSH: Democracy--United States. | Republicanism--United
    States. |
        Political culture--United States.
Classification: LCC JK1726 .H377 2022 | DDC 320.973--dc23/
    eng/20220218
LC record available at https://lccn.loc.gov/2021059401

Printed in the United States
0 9 8 7 6 5 4 3 2 1

Fulcrum Publishing
3970 Youngfield Street
Wheat Ridge, Colorado 80033
(800) 992-2908 • (303) 277-1623
www.fulcrumbooks.com

With loving memory of my
beloved wife, Lee

I.
THE AMERICAN REPUBLIC CAN SAVE AMERICAN DEMOCRACY

Restoration of the American Republic is vital now more than ever. For it is the qualities of the republic and the republican ideal that can save America's democratic values from the looming threat of authoritarianism.

This essay is not an extended academic comparison and contrast of republics and democracies. That is for college political history textbooks. Rather it is an explication of the factors that have characterized republics since ancient Rome and that carried forward through the era of the Enlightenment into the learned minds of America's Founders.

Those Founders chose the language and concepts of republicanism congenial to their historic creative process. A few of them, John Adams and Alexander Hamilton most notably, eschewed the notion of "democracy," thinking of it primarily in terms of dangerous mobs in the streets and the French Revolution.

After more than two centuries since our founding, it is nothing less than amazing that political discourse in America employs democratic language almost exclusively, and outside the academy few can be found, even among educated Americans, who can provide a brief, cogent description of a republic, this even though we salute the American flag and "the Republic for which it stands."

The case to be made here is that authoritarian forces are out to undermine and subvert the principles of democratic government, and the best defense of democracy is to be found, as our Founders knew, in the pillars of republican principles and ideals.

Although democracy has survived in America for more than 240 years, not always elegantly, the rise of populist nationalism here and in Europe and its increasing synchronization across the waters are evidence of potent threats that highlight democracy's vulnerability. The culprits are uniformly held to be globalization and its unfair distribution of benefits, increased distance between a small wealthy elite (Davos man) and middle-class wage earners, mass migrations south to north, stagnation of opportunity, alienation of everyday citizens from the political class, the consequent rise of the right, a tilt toward authoritarianism, and much else.

The rise of populist nationalism and its erosion of democracy is increasingly well documented but with little suggestion of how to save democracy.

Here, the confusion over whether America is a democracy or a Republic, or both, may offer a path. Earlier this year the *New York Times* reported on a squabble in Michigan over whether the United States was a republic or a democracy. Of course, it took Thomas Jefferson to coin the phrase "a democratic republic."

Our Founders proclaimed the new nation a Republic but one with a democratic form of government. It is timely to consider whether the former may save the latter.

II.
THE QUALITIES AND VIRTUES OF REPUBLICS

Whereas democracies focus on equality, justice, and other rights, the qualities of republics throughout history include popular sovereignty, a sense of the common good, resistance to corruption, and civic virtue.

We assume centers of power, and therefore political authority, to be in both Washington, D.C., politically, and New York, financially. Media power used to be centered in New York as well, at least until the advent of social media, which now seems centered in Silicon Valley.

Instead, in a Republic such as ours power is not located in these places. It is dispersed throughout the country. It belongs to us, *the people, who are sovereign* in this Republic. In this democracy we do routinely select representatives to promote and protect our individual and national interests. But they are ultimately accountable to us who are the sovereigns.

The greatest affirmation of popular sovereignty is found in the opening clause of our Constitution: "We the people…."

Autocracy, the denial of popular sovereignty, coalesces executive and legislative power in the hands of an individual who, including in our system, may also have the power to dictate those responsible for the judicial system. In the past few years, we have witnessed this dangerous trend.

Our sense of the *common good* wanes in ordinary times and waxes when we are threatened from abroad or our economy becomes depressed at home. Too many Americans have to be told about our intricate national security systems, interstate transportation systems, public lands and resources, research laboratories, monetary protections, and a very long list of institutions that belong to all of us and that keep our country interconnected.

In his *Discourses on Livy*, Machiavelli writes: "It is not the pursuit of individual good but of the common good that makes cities great, and it is beyond doubt that the common good is never considered except in republics" (quoted in *Liberty Before Liberalism*, Quentin Skinner, Cambridge University Press, 1998).

And *civic virtue*, the duty we all owe our Republic to participate in self-government at all levels, is perennially moribund. Complaints about our democracy are abundant. Efforts to make it better are faint.

In *Democracy's Discontents*, Professor Michael Sandel argues that the "first right" in a republic, above all those in the First Amendment, is "the right to govern ourselves." That requires civility, engagement, mutual respect, integrity, reason, and maturity. Without performance of the right of civic participation, all other rights are jeopardized.

Our failure to exercise our sovereign powers through protection of the common good—always threatened by persistent conservative efforts to privatize it—and through the exercise of civic virtue or civic engagement, starting always with the vote, weakens our resistance to corruption, the plague of republics throughout history.

Historians of the republic define corruption as placing special or personal interests ahead of the common good. Our national, state, and local governments are hotbeds of special pleadings and thus corrupt by this classical definition in ways much broader than bribery.

The Supreme Court decision in the *Citizens United* case made this massive corruption legal. The "golden rule" is now enshrined: he who has the most gold, rules. Arguably now the United States is well down the dangerous path that has corrupted all republics throughout history.

All citizens are accountable for the protection of their Republic whose flag we salute. Our Founders saw their newly created Republic as a bulwark against external threat and internal tyranny as well. James Madison, in *Federalist* 51, wrote: "It is of great importance in a republic not only to guard the society against the oppression of its rulers, but also to guard one part of the society against the injustice of the other part. If men were angels, no government would be necessary."

Imagine a reformation in which citizens began to exercise their sovereignty on a daily basis by demanding regular accounts of the health of the commonwealth, all those things we hold together and in trust for future generations. Imagine those same citizens taking an evening off from television to attend a city council or county commission meeting, a school board meeting, a parent-teacher evening, a candidate town hall speech, or even listening to a podcast on an issue of the day.

The republican ideal of a society closely knitted by a common history and a common good was reflected by the philosopher Charles Taylor, among many others: "Functioning republics are like families in this crucial respect, that part of what binds people together is their common history. Family ties or old friendships are deep because of what we have lived through together, and republics are bonded by time and climactic transitions" (*Philosophical Arguments*, Harvard University Press, 1995).

The effect of these duties of republican citizenship would drive the lobbyists and money changers in our halls of government into hiding. Broadly based citizen participation would do much to restrain the single-issue politics now dominating the public square and would greatly restore the standard of the national interest to legislative debate.

The movement politics in the twentieth century, for civil rights, equality for women, enlightened environmentalism, nuclear arms control, and increasingly to reverse climate destruction, are instances of citizens taking charge of public agendas and proof of popular sovereignty in action.

Demands for transparency and openness would substantially restore integrity to all levels of government in our Republic.

But they would also do much more to save democracy, our form of government.

Democracies protect rights. Republics promote duties. In a word, we must protect our rights by performance of our duties.

And despite the recent wholesale abandonment of traditional norms in government and politics, there are humanitarian efforts undertaken by civic-minded Americans at many levels. Consider the religious and private humanitarian efforts underway at our fraught southern border to aid separated families and children in need. Share Our Strength provides tens of millions of meals to hungry children. City Year, now AmeriCorps, for years has established urban projects for young people who receive education financing in return. First Book provides books to children whose homes have no books.

As a long-time advocate of public service for young people, particularly but not exclusively, much more should be done on behalf of democracy's flourishing to encourage young people after completing their education to consider a year or more of service in one or more levels of government, in community projects, as volunteers in nonprofit organizations or in humanitarian projects. The same observation includes retirees with time on their hands.

Such service responds to our Founders' use of the phrase "civic virtue," the contribution of time and energy to the common good locally, statewide, or nationally. Such public service makes a citizen of any age more aware of belonging to a community and a nation. It widens horizons beyond the commercial and money-making side of life.

For those in government service, at any level, public service shows what governments actually do day to day and the crucial functions career public servants perform for all the people. That experience also defeats the cynicism that prevails in many circles, including elements of the media, toward those who provide vital and important public services on a daily basis.

It would be beneficial if every generation of Americans heard a leader say, "Ask what you can do for your country."

These and many other projects like them are instances of civic engagement and civic virtue. They also do much to repair the damage done to our democracy by the selfish and unconcerned. But private charity and activism can never totally replace a democratic government committed to equality and justice for all.

Much public discontent and suppressed anger is due to the perception, and too often the reality, that laws are passed and high court rulings enacted to legitimize undemocratic systems at war with our Republic's principles and values. The Supreme Court decision in the *Citizens United* case, giving corporations First Amendment speech protection (namely, unlimited campaign contributions) stands as one of the worst examples of this trend.

Restoration of the early American republican ideal will by no means cure all the ills afflicting this democracy. America's geographic and demographic sweep, our massive internal mobility, the fragmentation of authority from the national to the city level all mitigate against the establishment of the stable, interconnected, mutually dependent polis identified with republics throughout the ages.

Indeed, it required Montesquieu to provide our Founders the solution to the issue of scope and scale the new nation faced in creating a truly national Republic. His solution: federation. A series of republics, each containing the historic republican attributes, could federate nationally while pursuing the republican ideal locally.

Still, democracy's discontents afflict our entire nation, and it is argued here that application of republican principles to those discontents offer the best hope of revitalizing and restoring a true national democratic Republic.

The links all trace to the citizen and the qualities of citizenship. As Rousseau observed: "There can be no patriotism without liberty, no liberty without virtue, no virtue without citizens."

The restoration of democracy through republican virtues leaves only unpleasant alternatives. The contemporary Italian republican theorist Maurizio Viroli writes this: "Republicanism has the historical and moral resources to revive or indeed engender civic enthusiasm, without a revelation of faith and without a dogmatic belief in history or in a leader. Either we shall find a way to reinforce republican politics and culture, or we shall have to resign ourselves to living in nations whose governments are controlled by the cunning and the arrogant" (*Republicanism*, Farrar, Straus and Giroux, 1999).

III.
UNDERSTANDING
THE REPUBLIC

As a graduate of public schools in Ottawa, Kansas, one of the eighth grade classes that I found most interesting was called Civics. In that class we discussed ideas such as citizenship, democracy, the public good, and most of all duty.

It all seemed self-evident but important. It was about what it meant to be an American, a citizen of a democracy. This was just a few years after the end of World War II, the earth-shaking events of which were still in our minds and made us, even at a relatively young age, conscious of the importance of democracy when fascism in Europe and Asia arose to represent the brutal use of power to slaughter tens of millions of people.

Although we ourselves were too young to fight, we all had fathers and uncles who did fight, and in many if not most families some came back badly wounded, in mind if not in body, or did not come back at all.

So, civics was not an abstraction. It had vivid meaning and large-scale consequences. Now, decades later, one does not hear of it being taught at all.

It might profitably be asked whether the disappearance of Civics classes had any connection with the unprecedented invasion of our nation's Capitol, destruction of the temple of democracy, and even search for a vice president and speaker of the house with murderous intent on that day that will live in infamy, January 6, 2021.

Still, eighth grade Civics was taught in the language of democracy even as we opened the school day by saluting the flag of the United States "and the Republic for which it stands."

It took several decades later and twelve years in the US Senate for me to ask the obvious question: What is a republic and why do we salute its flag?

We have already listed the qualities of a republic—popular sovereignty, a sense of the commonwealth, resistance to corruption, and, perhaps most important, what ancient Rome up through America's Founders called civic virtue.

Let's explore each of these at slightly greater length to build the case for our republican heritage saving our democracy.

A.
Popular Sovereignty

The *Oxford English Dictionary* defines sovereignty as "supreme, self-governing, royal." In historical usage, the sovereign was a monarch, a king.

Fourth century BC Romans produced the revolutionary notion that the *people* were the sovereigns. The people held the power, they were supreme, they could govern themselves. This became a cornerstone of early republican thought. Some scholars find threads of this concept as early as the eighth century BC.

One scholar cites a quote from an American Founder James Wilson to this effect: "When Homer listed the Greek forces who fought at Troy . . . he listed the Athenians as representing 'the people of Athens'" not a king (Carl J. Richard, *The Founders and the Classics*, Harvard University Press, 1995). Wilson later wrote: "The supreme power . . . *resides* in the *people*, as the fountain of government."

The theory of republics, from Rome through Venice, the Swiss cantons, disappearing until resurrected by Machiavelli in the fifteenth century, and then through the English and Scottish Enlightenments to the new American Republic, was that they had necessarily to be small if the people were to be sovereign.

The Americans, citing Montesquieu, solved the popular sovereignty problem of scope and scale by the obvious reliance on representation at the national and statewide level. But they, especially Thomas Jefferson, insisted that "the people" participate directly in local government, the structure closest to them and, Jefferson thought, the venue most important to them.

The point was: the people could not claim to be sovereign if they did not exercise that sovereignty where they could in their local communities and at the higher and larger levels exercise that sovereignty by electing representatives of their collective interests. In common terms that meant paying attention and *voting*.

Our Declaration of Independence, citing our "unalienable rights" including "life, liberty, and the pursuit of happiness," held that to secure these rights "governments are instituted among men, deriving their just powers from the consent of the governed." This is affirmation that the ultimate source of authority in a democratic republic is the people themselves.

It must be asked, are the people still sovereign if they do not vote? For if they do not vote, and choose not to exercise their power, someone else will take it from them.

In the continuing chaos in the aftermath of the 2020 national election and early threats raised to expand that chaos by sidestepping the constitutional process for appointment of electors based on the popular vote, nothing less than the sanctity of the ballot and sovereignty of the people are at stake.

The essence of democracy is the preeminence of the popular vote, and the guarantee of the popular vote is the sovereignty of people, not state legislatures beholden to a party or faction. This is one of several arguments as to how the American Republic can save American democracy.

Popular sovereignty is the adhesive that binds the Republic and democracy together. But that adhesive is threatened by manipulation of popular vote counts; and removal of authority from the people is democracy's greatest threat. And it is looming.

That is why so much attention was paid in the founding of the American Republic to two equally important pillars of the new structure: the common interest and corruption.

B.
The Sense of
a Commonwealth

Back to the *Oxford English Dictionary*. A commonwealth is "an independent state or community." Pennsylvania, Virginia, and several other states consider themselves as commonwealths. But the definition has evolved over time to include common interests and concerns, all those tangible and intangible things we Americans hold in common, as contrasted with special, subordinate interests.

We hold more things in common than most Americans realize. The list is very long but includes, among much else, our national security forces, our national parks and recreation areas, our public transportations systems—including our interstate highway systems—public research centers, public health systems, public education institutions administered by states and local communities, the postal service, and, of course, our environment, our air and water, and public lands.

Take some time to list many more components of the American commonwealth.

With the exception of our military forces and structures, there are perennial efforts to privatize all this and more for profit-making purposes. But why should private corporations own and control what we all now own together? This is an extreme to which all but the most ardent capitalists will not go.

Because republics throughout history, beginning with the early Romans and to a lesser degree the Greeks, have understood, as did our Founders, that shared public concerns and institutions were central to the ideal of the republic and required republican citizens to acknowledge and participate in their ownership.

Otherwise, the republic will fall into disrepair and interest groups will take over. Common interests will first be forgotten and then disappear.

The commonwealth brings us together. It is an acknowledgment that we have more in common than we have interests that drive us apart. There is no such thing as a republic of special interests and an atom-ized citizenry. The commonwealth is another aspect of the glue that keeps a disparate republic together.

There is a strong moral component to the commonwealth concept. That is the sacred steward-ship we owe our children. In abstract theory, we could privatize much of the commonwealth and pay off the national debt.

But, then what? What do we leave our chil-dren? We have a sacred duty to care not only for ourselves but also for future generations. They have a genuine interest in a commonwealth and the repub-lic that supports it. We may leave a balanced budget for one generation but in exchange lose our security, natural resources, transportation systems, and our environment and climate.

The Preamble to our Constitution makes our stewardship of our commonwealth a sacred duty by stating that its purpose is to "secure the blessings of liberty to ourselves *and our posterity*." Thus, the commonwealth is multigenerational. Our responsi-bilities for preserving the commonwealth extend to those yet unborn. And what we preserve is not just our natural heritage but also the principles of service and duty upon which the American Republic is founded.

That is why a sense of the commonwealth and the common good has been at the center of every true republic throughout history. Without it, the republic is no longer a republic.

That is also why my neighbors and I find it necessary to coalesce formally and informally to protect and promote our common interests and shared heritage. Each of us cannot protect our most valuable assets by ourselves. The sense of a commonwealth compels us to pull together to promote our common interests. That is what makes a republic a republic while, at the same time, saving the democratic process of freedom and rights for each other.

In theory, we can privatize some of our national legacy. But, if we do, we will no longer be able to salute the flag of "the Republic for which it stands."

The every-man-for-himself idea may sound rugged and individualistic, but it soon devolves in cultural fragmentation and social clashes. There have been too many instances where this theory has been tried and found seriously wanting and dangerous.

In a 1989 book entitled *Albion's Seed*, the American historian David Hackett Fischer traces the early colonialist from different areas of England, Scotland, and Ireland to specific settlements on the American continent. The English Cavaliers, for example, largely settled in what became the Commonwealth of Virginia. The Quakers settled in the Delaware Valley. The Scotch-Irish arranged themselves along Appalachia and into the border colonies. The Puritans by and large settled in the northeast that became New England.

And each of these distinctive colonies brought with them their own cultural characteristics that linger, sometimes strongly, even today some three centuries after. The Puritans of New England practiced communal responsibility, government institutions, and adherence to law. The Cavaliers built a society of concentrated wealth and great estates populated by leading families served by slavery. The Scotch-Irish of the southern mountains and hill country were fiercely independent, resisted imposed authority, emphasized self-reliance, and populated early America's frontier.

Professor Fischer's thesis is fascinating, especially if many of those distinctive tribal traits and characteristics explain striking political and cultural divisions that persist so many decades, even centuries, later.

In many ways, these strong cultural characteristics might explain why America as a republic, with its sense of the commonwealth, has been so difficult to perpetuate. It also may account for the more universal acceptance of the United States as a democracy with its rights and freedoms rather than a republic of citizen duties, responsibilities, and obligations, a distinction discussed more elaborately in the following, but one central to the thesis of this essay.

If we wish to restore our Republic as a means to protect our democracy, the sense that we inhabit a shared commonwealth, with more that binds us together rather than drives us apart, is essential.

We have had periods, especially in the last century, when internal and external events brought us together as a nation. At home, we all experienced the Great Depression of the late 1920s and throughout the 1930s. We have enshrined that era with nostalgic songs and stories. We were all in it together.

One of my most vivid early memories is of my hardworking mother handing out sugar sandwiches, a slice of bread with a very thin layer of butter and a sprinkling of sugar, to men of the road who jumped off standing railcars on the tracks behind our house. They were all thin, wearing overalls and worn work shirts, and deeply grateful. As meager as our life was, they could not be turned away. We were all in this together.

Americans inhabited a commonwealth of poverty during the Great Depression.

Thereafter, we were quickly brought together by the shared experience of World War II. It was a boon to profiteers and black-market manipulators, but more importantly almost every American family was touched directly or indirectly by the draft of 12 million young Americans, virtually overnight, too many of whom never came home or returned with a serious physical or mental illness.

We inhabited a commonwealth of sacrifice. And few complained.

Throughout the good times and the bad, the question of who could and should participate in the commonwealth persisted. And here is where the tracks of American democracy intersect with the tracks of the Republic.

In the mid-nineteenth century we fought a bitter and bloody Civil War over preservation of the Union and liberation of enslaved Black Americans. Women had to struggle for decades to earn the right to vote, and only then in the early twentieth century. Working people fought for decades to secure the right to form unions. Young people during the Vietnam era protested that they could not vote even as they were being drafted, and they finally prevailed.

It is a matter of more than curiosity why so many, including those who talk the loudest about freedoms and rights of democracy, are also those most resistant to opening the gates of the commonwealth to those left behind.

On many dimensions, the history of America is the history of the expansion of the right of participation in our national commonwealth.

C.
Resistance
to Corruption

Say "corruption" to most Americans, and they instinctively think bribery, especially within the precinct of politics. But that is only a small part of it. And most of that we have learned to cope with by laws and honest prosecutors.

From early Rome onward, republicanism has pursued a different definition. Corruption has been used to describe placing individual or special interests ahead of the common good in governing structures.

By that much broader definition, twenty-first century American government is massively corrupt.

The army of lobbyists in Washington expands regardless of which political party is in power in the White House or the Houses of Congress. Neither party is less corrupt than the other.

It must be said that some interests, with lobbyists of their own, are less greedy than others. Most of us would make a distinction between the interests of nurses or schoolteachers or public service employees and those of energy companies, financial institutions, or yacht owners.

Although interests are often about money, there is a difference between a small salary increase for an overworked nurse and the corporate profits and annual salaries of corporate executives. These are social value questions that must be considered in assessing the degree to which an interest erodes the structure of and confidence in a republic.

But all special interest pleading, usually behind closed doors, does not take place in the nation's Capitol alone. Every state government and, indeed, every city government, and in the case of local development, every zoning authority is subject to special pleading, sometimes also behind closed doors.

The incestuous corruption of republican government at all these levels is compounded by two other factors: campaign contributions and the revolving door.

Most Americans are aware of the connection between the special interest and its lobbyists and contributions to the election or reelection of a national, state, or local officeholder. It would be absurd to deny the connection between a special interest campaign contribution and the position of a candidate or officeholder on that interest's concern.

Since the lobbying industry—and it is a huge industry—has itself grown so large and powerful, any wish to dissolve it is a dream (or perhaps nightmare). The principal corrective is now found in more or less effective reports by political campaigns. Filings are required for candidates for national office reporting on contributions of more than nominal amounts. The same is true in some but not all states. In some cases, reports on last minute contributions come after the election.

The theory, of course, is that it is up to the voters themselves to decide whether there is a direct or indirect connection between large-scale contributions from special interests and the votes of the elected official. That is not nothing. But it presumes a level of citizen attention that often does not exist.

Sadly, it is easier to conclude that the whole system is corrupt than to take the time and trouble to try to correct it by paying attention.

But the system that presently prevails is one of subtle legalized bribery. The single-most significant contributor to this system is the astonishing costs of television and radio advertising. It is not uncommon for a network or local electronic media outlet to decry the astonishing amount of money spent on campaigns even as that outlet rakes in the profits.

But the most powerful interest groups have other cards up their sleeves in the form of the "revolving door." They hire former officeholders, including elected officials and those who have held high level appointive positions, to represent their interests.

Former elected officials have (the magic word in politics) *access* to their former colleagues. They can open doors, call upon old friendships, find time on the calendar, and, of course, wine and dine.

One recent report in the *New York Times* documented a significant number of senior officials in the US Department of the Treasury in the previous Trump administration who resigned after the 2020 national election and took up senior positions in some of the largest investment firms in the nation with a substantial increase in their personal incomes. They took with them not only access to old colleagues but also, more importantly, intimate knowledge of complex regulations of the financial industry of crucial importance to those firms. This meant they knew how to take advantage of or circumvent the very regulations that former public officials had written.

It is all about money. And that money is corrupt by the classic definition of corruption characterized by republics throughout history.

That is why resistance to this kind of corruption has been so crucial to the survival of those historic republics and why it is now so dangerous to the American Republic.

Steps can and should be taken. There can be statutory prohibitions against former elected and appointed officials from representing interests before the Congress or regulatory agencies for a year or more. Elaborate schemes to hide the true source of special interest campaign contributions as originating from obscure political action committees can be dissolved, and greater transparency of the sources of contributions can be enacted.

In sum, the ability of the American Republic to save American democracy through popular sovereignty, the common good, and civic virtue are compromised by special interest corruption—putting wealthy and powerful interests ahead of the common good.

This may be the reason we do not learn about or discuss the character of our Republic, although we salute its flag. We are too busy looking out for ourselves instead of each other and future generations.

D.
Civic Virtue as
Civic Duty

This phrase, so important to believers in the republic from the ancients to our own Founders is used only infrequently in modern times. This is in part because of the decline of civic education generally, as discussed earlier, but also because we are not clear how "virtue" is defined in the civic context.

In the early republics, the phrase "civic virtue" was meant to connote investment of time and energy in promoting the common good, exercising popular sovereignty, and resisting corruption. Today, we substitute words such as "participation," "engagement," and "involvement" in some or all levels of self-government, from the local school board to national and even international affairs.

This requires keeping up with the daily news, suspect these days because of highly partisan media; discussing current affairs with family, friends, and neighbors; attending political candidate events and town meetings; asking questions of those in authority; in short, paying attention and keeping informed.

Contrary to partisan apologists, those who practice violence and hatred and destroy public property up to and including waging insurrection against the institutions of national government are not exercising free speech and are far from exercising civic virtue.

Virtue has its basis in morality. To lack virtue is to be worthless and ineffective.

Let's consider reasons for the decline of the ancient value of virtue. We have discussed the failure of civic education in our school systems. It is enlightening to a young student to learn that our system of government is most effective when citizens are informed and actively participate in public forums. It is further enlightening to know that our Constitution, particularly its First Amendment, encourages and protects that participation through a free press, public assembly, and free speech.

Family dinner table discussions once were the most immediate forums for parents to discuss public events with their children. But then came television, new forms of family structures, and, alas, too many parents who were not up-to-date enough to engage in discussions or simply didn't care. Distraction replaced engagement.

But here is exactly where republican principles intersect with democratic rights. Participation in the American Republic's institutions of government involve citizen duties. If we wish to save our Republic we must participate. And it is through that activity of participation that we can best protect our democracy and secure our rights.

To neglect the obligation, the *duty* side of the coin endangers the *rights* side of the coin.

This is critical, because our democracy is under assault at its most vulnerable point, free and fair elections. Efforts are now underway in at least a dozen and a half states to suppress citizens' rights to vote. By unnecessarily increasing restrictions on voter registration, reducing voting hours, reducing voting places, increasing voter identification requirements, reducing or eliminating absentee and mail-in voting provisions, and other barriers, democracy's doors are being closed.

Our Founders, especially Thomas Jefferson, were concerned that our new Republic, whose scope and scale far surpassed any republic in history, provided insufficient avenues for citizen participation. But they knew that the one avenue that would remain open was the opportunity to vote, an opportunity even then secured to white men and in some cases only those who owned land.

The history of America is one of struggle to expand the franchise. Now forces are at work to contract it once again.

But the forces of voter suppression are also at work to limit those who can *count* the ballots. The forces of manipulation in those dozen and a half states are carefully appointing and electing election officials at the precinct up to the statewide levels who will make sure, often behind closed doors, that their favored candidates prevail.

Thus, they are shamelessly using false allegations of voter fraud to carry out voter fraud.

The goal of this antidemocratic scheme is to enable friendly state legislatures to appoint electors for the presidency without regard to the popular vote, if necessary, to achieve their favored outcome.

Should this manipulative scheme succeed, it will mark the end of America's central democratic pillar, the ballot, and the rise of authoritarian government. Nothing less than this is at stake.

This is why it is argued here that only by the restoration of republican principles, including popular sovereignty, a sense of the commonwealth, resistance to corruption, and civic duty, can we save democracy and our democratic rights.

I once had the occasion to sit next to former President Richard Nixon at a funeral service in New York. We briefly discussed exchanging essays and he said, "You know, nothing is free."

As American citizens, our democratic rights are free. But we must protect them by performance of our duties as prescribed by our Republic.

One must tread lightly when using a word like "duty" to many Americans. It sounds too much like coercion, and that is something governments do. "Don't tread on me," as the well-known New Hampshire motto says.

Many of these same people have happily joined the pro-authoritarian tendency now projecting itself across the country. If these same people don't like coercion, wait until they find out how authoritarianism works.

In any case, as used in this context, duty it not something ordered for you to do by the government. It is a sense of true citizenship that causes you to *want* to participate in government and causes important to the nation, its society, and future generations.

Decent people consider it a responsibility to care for their parents, but they don't feel it is a duty. It is something done out of affection, concern, and care. The same is true in raising our children. Caring for them requires us to perform tasks out of obligation to them and their well-being. We shovel snow from our elderly neighbor's sidewalk. We don't have to. But we do it because it gives us satisfaction and makes us feel good about ourselves. That feeling is virtue. And it is its own reward.

It is a cause for wonder that those who often proclaim themselves to be bigger and better patriots than their neighbor who may belong to a different political party are often the first to say I'm voting against the mill levy for the badly needed new school or climate change is a hoax.

We are quick to weep at the new grave of a fallen soldier but do not think there are even the smallest civic obligations we should expect of ourselves. Get out of my way. I'm an American.

The best duty is the one done voluntarily and without expectation of reward except the sense that you have done something good for the right reason.

In this essay, that is the way the idea of duty is put forward. We save democracy because democracy has given us the greatest nation on earth.

And it seems to this American that the surest way to preserve and protect democracy is to restore the principles of the republic. Popular sovereignty. A sense of the common good. Resistance to corruption. And civic duty.

If the American people have the ultimate power, then we stand up against the current autocratic tendency being foisted upon us by a small group of power-hungry plotters.

We secure and perpetuate our sovereignty by protecting all those things we hold in common. We remind ourselves frequently that generations of far-sighted leaders in days gone by had the foresight to create and protect our common interests, and that we must preserve and protect those interests in sacred trust for our children and generations yet unborn.

But we must constantly remind ourselves also that corruption is the greatest enemy of republics, ours as well as others that have succumbed over the centuries. And common bribery is only a small aspect of corruption. The republic-killing corruption that we must arm against is the replacement of the common good with special interests. This currently is one of the greatest dangers faced by the Republic of America.

"We are creating a Republic," said Benjamin Franklin outside Philadelphia's Constitution Hall, "if you can keep it."

I fear we are not keeping it. I fear we are in danger of losing it, to the authoritarians and the special interests supporting them by undermining the common good.

Let's consider some examples of all these dangers.

In the discussion earlier on resistance to corruption, I cite a recent *New York Times* article ("How Accounting Giants Craft Favorable Tax Rules from Inside Government," September 19, 2021) regarding the "revolving door" between giant accounting firms and the US Treasury Department through which pass high level employees of the firms who receive appointments to even higher-level positions at

Treasury. Here, they write rules and regulations on highly complex but also highly lucrative financial practices and then, after a year or two, return to their former employers as very high salaried partners advising large business clients on how to take advantage of the rules and regulations they drafted.

From the *Times*:

The largest U.S. accounting firms have perfected a remarkably effective behind-the-scenes system to promote their interests in Washington. Their tax lawyers take senior jobs at the Treasury Department, where they write policies that are frequently favorable to their former corporate clients, often with the expectation they will soon return to their old employers. The firms welcome them back with loftier titles and higher pay. . . . From their government posts, many of the industry veterans approved loopholes long exploited by their former firms, gave tax breaks to former clients and rolled back efforts to rein in tax shelters—with enormous impact.

This revolving door is used by both political parties but more recently and more blatantly by Republican administrations.

Once again a quote from a leading tax lawyer in the *Times*: "The accounting firms have a desire to get in favorable rules for their clients. And the person in the government has a desire to grant their wish because they know they will be rewarded when they get out." As the *Times* notes, this is nothing new. "But the ability of the world's largest accounting firms to embed their top lawyers inside the government's most important tax-policy jobs has largely escaped public scrutiny."

Often these private lawyers take a large pay cut to take the government position, but they receive significantly higher pay when they return, within a year or two, to their original firms.

Sadly, the revolving door often characterizes every government agency and the industries they regulate across the entire government. Often, the person going through the revolving door into the private sector he or she was just regulating is a former member of Congress who also will receive a pay boost of two, three, or more times his or her congressional salary.

This is relevant to this discussion of the republic primarily because it shows the danger of corruption but also because the corruption erodes the public's confidence in their government. That loss of confidence encourages public cynicism and opens the door to demagogues inciting violent insurrection against the government and protests to replace democracy with authoritarianism.

The republican ideal of popular sovereignty is already badly eroded by an era of assassinations, partisan media, single-issue causes, false claims of fraudulent elections, terrorist threats, military invasions based on false arguments, and partisan bickering, among much else.

Our government is elected to carry out the will of the people. But, as argued here, public confidence in government has been consciously and willfully eroded by partisans whose only goal is power for its own sake.

There were no nuclear weapons in Iraq, but our leaders lied to us and even to each other.

Loss of confidence by the people in their government involves high costs, including perhaps most importantly confidence in our national security.

What good are all the hundreds of billions of dollars a year spent on our military and intelligence systems if members of Congress, including from a political party that used to consider itself "strong on defense," publicly berate and undermine the authority of senior military commanders?

We regret to think what a poll today would show in answer to a question: Do you have confidence in the government you have elected to serve you?

The people cannot be sovereigns in a country whose government they don't trust.

The linkage between popular sovereignty and resistance to corruption is clear. And it does center on the public trust.

Closing the revolving door, at least for a time after leaving public office, would go far to reestablish that trust and to strengthen the role of the republic in protecting democracy.

It would also reestablish popular sovereignty, the power of the people to insist on integrity in government, their government. And among the duties of citizenship is the need to hold elected and appointed officeholders to account. An essential element of corruption is public neglect of accountability.

Corruption hates the spotlight of public attention. This also is the responsibility of the press whose freedom is guaranteed by the First Amendment. For every tangent of celebrity and gossip, real corruption slips by unattended.

A national government of, for, and by the people, not a host of special interests, is necessary in a Republic such as ours but also necessary to secure our democracy against corrosion and corruption.

We have also seen the close connection between civic education and civic duty. Engaged, participating, and involved citizens will not permit their republic to become corrupted by special interests. Simply paying attention, even at the local level, is the best guarantee against government manipulation, favoritism, and behind-the-scenes deal making.

It does take time, but it is more than worth the effort for the reward of integrity in government. Failure to participate and ask direct questions produces widespread cynicism among citizens and drives a wedge between them and all levels of their government. Widespread participation, however, has the opposite effect. It brings citizens together and strengthens the sense of the commonwealth, the sense that we are all in this together.

To protect our democracy, our guarantee of rights and freedoms, our Republic must be strong, vibrant, and resilient. Power, ultimate power, must be in the hands of the people. The people as sovereigns must understand and protect the commonwealth, our collective heritage held in sacred trust for future generations. And the people as sovereigns will prevent special interests from corrupting our commonwealth and our government, which oversees it.

All of this, the qualities of the republic, are dependent on citizen duties. Once again it is necessary to stress that the duties of love, one's family, friends, and neighbors, are not tedious obligations. They are opportunities and blessings to be able to help others whom one cares about. The same is true of our nation, our commonwealth, that we claim to honor and care about.

The duties of citizenship are slight by comparison to the blessings of liberty, security, and the bonds of citizen friendships in America. Tens of millions of people dream of being in America. Very few Americans dream of living elsewhere.

The first duty in our democratic Republic is to *vote*. It should not be surprising to any American that authoritarians are suppressing votes and voters. They do not want *the people* to participate, only those most likely to support them. We require new citizens to take an oath to "support and defend the Constitution." Those of us born here are not required to take that oath.

To avoid confusion, it is necessary to consider the phrase "civic virtue" further, in part because it is a phrase rarely found in modern political discourse, and where the word "virtue" is used it is almost always in reference to a personal, not a public, quality.

One scholar writing in a book entitled *Civic Virtues,* provides this explanation: "The virtuous citizen must be free, but not simply free to go his or her own way. Instead, the citizen is free when he or she participates in the government of his or her community. As part of the community, the citizen will recognize that the government of common affairs is more or less directly self-government. If self-government requires the occasional sacrifice of one's personal interests, so be it, for the sacrifice is necessary not only in the name of civic duty but also in order to preserve the liberties of the citizen of a self-governing polity. That, then, is what civic virtue was—and still is, according to those theorists who want to revive the republican spirit in contemporary politics" (*Civic Virtues*, Richard Dagger, Oxford University Press, 1997).

During the early debates on the American Revolution, John Adams took up the distinction between civic virtue and private virtue. "The classical republican heritage embraced by the Revolutionaries," writes Drew McCoy, "stressed the close relationship between public virtue—the austere and unselfish devotion to the common good that was on the lips of every patriot in 1776—and private virtue, which was exemplified by the character traits of frugality, temperance, and rigorous self-control." He then cites a letter from John Adams a few months before the Declaration of Independence: "Public virtue cannot exist in a Nation without Private, and public Virtue is the only Foundation of Republics" (*The Elusive Republic*, Drew R. McCoy, University of North Carolina Press, 1980).

It is finally left to James Madison in the *Federalist* to take up the central role of virtue in the proposed new American Republic: "I go on this great republican principle, that the people will have virtue and intelligence to select men of virtue and wisdom. Is there no virtue among us? If there be not, we are in a wretched situation. No theoretical checks, no form of government can render us secure. To suppose that any form of government will secure liberty or happiness without any virtue in the people is a chimerical idea" (quoted in *The Ideological Origins of the American Revolution*, Bernard Bailyn, Harvard University Press, 1967).

Similarly, the notion of corruption, the bane of all republics throughout history, has gone, as mentioned earlier, through a distinct shrinkage of meaning since first warned against by early Roman writers and speakers. For them, and virtually all republican thinkers since then, corruption was the act of placing personal or special interests ahead of the common good. Today, as discussed, it is mostly confined to descriptions of bribery.

One of the most profound scholars on republican theory today, Professor Quentin Skinner, cites Machiavelli to the effect that we generally "tend to be 'corrupt', a term of art the republican theorists habitually use to denote our natural tendency to ignore the claims of our community as soon as they seem to conflict with the pursuit of our own immediate advantage."

Professor Skinner then goes on to say, "To be corrupt . . . is to forget—or fail to grasp—something which is profoundly in our interests to remember: that if we wish to enjoy as much freedom as we can hope to obtain within political society, there is good reason for us to act in the first instance as virtuous citizens, placing the common good above the pursuit of any individual or factional ends" (*Machiavelli and Republicanism*, Gisela Bock, Quentin Skinner, and Maurizio Viroli, Cambridge University Press, 1990).

Another scholar put the image more vividly. Contrasting today's usage as bribery or embezzlement, "For seventeenth and eighteenth century thinkers . . . the word [corruption] more often brought to mind a fuller, more coherent, and more dreadful image of a spreading rot . . . an organic cancer" (*The Jeffersonian Persuasion*, Lance Banning, Cornell University Press, 1978).

There are no republics in their 2,500-year history that have succumbed to corruption and survived.

This brief survey now makes it apparent that the qualities of a republic are profoundly interrelated. For sovereignty, governing power, to rest with the people, the citizens of a republic, they must place the commonwealth, the people's common good and interest, foremost. And they must collectively resist the constant cancer of corruption, the appeal of individual, special interests over the collective interests of the commonwealth.

If and only if, and this is the critical test, we can restore the American Republic to the status envisioned by our Founders, then and only then the qualities of our Republic can help us defeat the anti-democratic authoritarian forces now operating to end democracy in America.

IV.

THE THREATS TO
AMERICAN DEMOCRACY

A.
The American Republic
and Democracy

In common usage, we refer to our democracy as guaranteeing equal rights, we find its constitutional base in the First Amendment. Until recently we assumed democracy protected free and fair elections, and that elections were decided by a majority of the electoral vote. We equated democracy with civil rights, we saw it as the basis for political participation; democracy was the guarantor of transparency in government, basically democracy was a composite of a set of rules and norms by which we govern ourselves.

What has happened to challenge all these traditional beliefs and understandings? In times past, for example the so-called McCarthy era of the mid-twentieth century, undemocratic practices have arisen and been challenged in the judicial system and the court of public opinion. And in each case, American democracy has triumphed, and our systems were restored to their normal course.

Extremes of right and left are often associated with deviations from the democratic path. There have been socialist movements, with occasional violence such as in the 1920s. More often than not, these deviations have been on the right, such as domestic movements to support Hitler and fascism led by leading American figures such as Henry Ford and Charles Lindbergh in the 1930s. Sometimes, such as in the McCarthy era, communism was seen as a threat to America, which the pro-Hitler forces used to justify their rightward arguments.

They chose Hitler over Stalin, as if that were the only choice.

But, in recent years a new antidemocratic movement representing vague authoritarian characteristics has arisen. And it is against this movement that this argument for the restoration of the American Republic is raised.

Its characteristics are concentration of power in a single executive, the president, backed by a political party dominated by that figure's will and unquestioning loyalty to it, a Congress that acts as a rubber stamp for that individual's actions and commands, and theatrical leadership displays reminiscent of European fascist leaders in the 1930s and 1940s.

Most recently, we are experiencing blatant authoritarianism by the Donald Trump–led charges that the 2020 election, which he lost, was "rigged," and that Trump himself was actually elected. Because there is no evidence of this, and courts have rejected such arguments routinely out of hand, the centerpiece of a democracy, free and fair elections, is mocked and undercut.

To the degree there is some kind of theory in all this charade, it must be that rejection of traditional political practices, ideals, and norms will necessarily lead to concentration of power in the hands of the authoritarian leader and his party that will do his bidding.

Mass anger and frustration is rarely generated out of whole cloth. The foundations of the current authoritarian movement are routinely attributed to globalization, the loss of manufacturing employment to competition, mass migrations south to north that overwhelm conventional immigration systems, racial conflicts brought on by immigration, a climate crisis running ahead of international policies to stop it, terrorism, and much else.

Authoritarianism says that traditional politics can and will solve none of this and that only a "strong" leader can do so. The strong leader's solutions are always simple, draconian, and wrong.

They are wrong simply because they require operations outside the bounds of democracy. The rights of individual citizens and peaceful assemblies are pushed aside or overridden. Unfavorable publications and news outlets are marginalized in favor of those who promote the leader's simple, and wrong, message; elections are determined not by the popular vote but rather by election officials and partisan assemblies who determine the predictable outcome.

All of this today and much more cause those who cherish our democratic principles and institutions to search for and suggest ideas to frustrate the authoritarian movement and protect the historic values of our nation.

And it is in that spirit that this essay, founded on the notion of restoration of our Republic, is suggested as one of the ways, and perhaps the best way, to save American democracy.

The best argument for this thesis is to apply the qualities of the republic discussed earlier to the immediate challenges to American democracy.

This argument is self-reinforcing. First, restoring *popular sovereignty*, the ideal that power in a republic belongs to the people, immediately and strongly negates any bizarre notion that what is needed is to concentrate political power in a single individual and the party of true believers that support him.

These two approaches are diametrically opposed. Republics throughout history have always stood in opposition to polities headed by kings, dictators, or authoritarians. That is why the republic was devised—to thwart the focus on concentrated power and to disburse responsibility among the people at large or through their elected representatives.

In short, should the authoritarian movement in America succeed in its aims, we can no longer refer to the American Republic or salute the flag for which it stands.

Popular sovereignty, by its very nature, demands free distribution of ideas, free assembly to discuss those ideas, and free speech to express one's position on the issues of the day. Authoritarian regimes rarely countenance any of this.

An authoritarian America, post-Republic, will require the First Amendment to the Constitution to be rewritten in specific restrictive terms. An authoritarian, post-Republic America will be a much different country. The control of the outcome of elections, regardless of the outcome of the vote, is the first and most important step toward dictatorship.

It is critical at this time of considerable danger to democracy for individual American citizens to participate in and engage with the institutions of government, and most of all express their desire to hold elected and appointed public officials at all levels of government accountable to the will of the people.

Especially important at this time is vigorous response to unsubstantiated and undocumented allegations of fraud in elections, as well as to the appointment of rigid partisans to local and state election positions in response to the alleged fraud but empowered to commit frauds of their own.

According to election experts, many of whom have publicly expressed deep concern, even fear, about manipulation of election systems in a dozen and a half conservative or borderline states, a silent coup is underway to predetermine the outcome of 2022 and 2024 elections. This can only succeed if millions of citizens of the American Republic forfeit their sovereignty and sit on the sidelines.

The forces of authoritarianism are militant, interconnected, determined, and opposed to our democracy and the Republic upon which it is based. There is limited organized counterweight to these forces.

Democratic forces are diverse, scattered, and unorganized. Authoritarian forces are single-minded, focused, and determined.

This is thus the fate of republics throughout history. In this respect, one might conclude that the American Republic is virtually unique. It represents not only the triumph of democracy but also the triumph of the republican form of government with little precedent in human history.

But in times of stress, and we are in one of those times, our Republic is being tested as never before. If forces of authority and concentrated power prevail, we will enter a new and much different chapter in America's life, and few will welcome it.

Our belief in the *commonwealth*, all we own and hold together, is also at stake. The powerful and wealthy interests supporting the authoritarian movement have much at stake in terms of their own financial interests.

An authoritarian state will be strongly inclined to reward its wealthy supporters with public resources now owned by the American people, including specifically our public lands, minerals, waterways, and timber. Through decades of public ownership and management the American people have benefited greatly through careful leasing of these resources, and fees collected have not only gone to pay for resource management but also education, health, housing, and much else. In a new authoritarian state, those resources plus transportation systems, recreation areas, and other publicly owned elements of the commonwealth will be privatized for private profit.

The fees you pay for the use of these elements of today's commonwealth will go into private treasuries and will not be used for the public good. Likewise, any prayer for a fair tax system will be abandoned once and for all.

The idea of the United States as a commonwealth will be strange to some, but through all those things we share and own together that is what we are. And, like popular sovereignty, the commonwealth ideal is part of the definition of what it means to be citizens of the American Republic. The ideal of the commonwealth ought to unite us, it should bring us together as co-owners of the public domain and facilities that belong to all of us. That many Americans do not know this is yet one more casualty of the demise of civic education.

Early on, our children should learn the meaning of our commonwealth. It is a vital part of being an American. It encompasses the common good. The authoritarian state does not recognize a commonwealth, including the one it replaces. Public resources are owned and controlled by the state and disbursed to its friends.

The destruction of any sense of the commonwealth is necessary for authoritarians because, having destroyed popular sovereignty, they do not want the populous to think of the common good and common interests. Those who think of owning public resources with their neighbors and fellow citizens are inevitably resistant to concentrated power at the top.

Likewise, authoritarians are intrinsically *corrupt*. Almost by instinct, they consider their own political power and the special interests supporting it as their due. To argue for the common good over narrow, special interests is a tautology for authoritarians.

A central goal of the authoritarian state is to pick and choose the interests to be promoted and served. Those would inevitably be the interests that promoted and supported the authoritarian government and helped bring it into being.

With authoritarianism, having dismantled popular sovereignty and destroyed the sense of the commonwealth, it is axiomatic that the corruption that destroys republicanism itself would be enshrined.

All of which means that even the idea of *civic virtue* is totally out of place in the authoritarian state. If the authoritarians replace democracy in America, any mention of civic duty or citizen involvement or participation will be the object of humor and scorn.

The title of virtuous will be reserved only for those who support the autocratic rulers. Those democratic and republican idealists from ancient

Athens and Rome forward will be dismissed out of hand as anathema to the new postdemocratic regime.

The neo-autocrat will deem himself virtuous. Most autocrats do. As he presents his own Oscar for virtuosity to himself, he will be applauded only by his own puppets handpicked for the occasion.

The new authoritarians do not waste time with subtlety. Their ultimate leaders place hour-long phone calls to state officials asking for manufactured votes. They are not set back by judges who dismiss their claims of voting fraud for absolute lack of evidence. Their legal representatives lack intelligence, experience, wit, and even cunning. They gleefully ransack the US Department of Justice as if it were their own private law firm. They appoint senior officials who have no idea what the department they are supposed to manage does or is supposed to do.

Competence, not to mention loyalty to the nation, are not high on the list of authoritarian qualities.

B.
The Rule of Law

The surest signs of creeping authoritarianism are avoidance of standard legal processes, short-circuiting of legal standards and practices, and most vividly the resort to force and violence rather than the judicial system.

Laws and legal rules and systems are the backbone of democracies. Where democracy is under fire from authoritarian attack, the courts and laws are the first to erode and be eroded.

Early in the Trump administration evidence began to mount of casual disregard of legal norms and procedures. The new president showed little sign of understanding the structure and functions of the national government he was elected to manage.

The Department of Defense was led by "my generals," he said. He suggested each of his children be given a federal agency or department to manage. Cabinet positions went to political supporters regardless of their expertise in the workings of their respective departments. To a person cabinet officers disregarded and paid little heed to career civil servants who had spent much of a lifetime overseeing specialized government functions.

Faced with mounting evidence, and leaks from inside departments and agencies that the senior appointed cabinet officer and his or her deputies knew little if anything of their constitutional duties, resignations, usually triggered by a scandal, began to occur with increasing rapidity. Incompetence is one thing; malfeasance is quite another. So, many first-round appointments left one step ahead of the hangman, in this case a federal prosecutor.

But this was confusing to the president. Did not those prosecutors work for *him*? Was not the US Department of Justice *his* law firm? Was he not only commander in chief of the US military, but also of the system of justice in America?

As a veteran of the Department of Justice in my early legal career, it was then the pinnacle of legal practice on behalf of the interests of the people of the United States. Its legal ranks, especially of career lawyers in the department, were impeccable and above reproach. It was uniformly considered an honor to have an appointment to the department. Its integrity was assumed and guaranteed. When politically appointed attorneys general and their assistants came to their offices without the shining legal résumés of their predecessors, career lawyers were dismayed.

If you wish to undermine democracy with authoritarianism, you must first compromise its legal structures. For democracies, not autocracies, are founded on law and the rule of law. The process of democracy destruction requires the rule of law to be undermined and then abandoned.

The increasing churning of politically appointed senior personnel in the departments and agencies was soon mirrored in the White House itself. Chiefs of staff and national security advisors came and went through their own revolving door. Some resigned, others were fired by a president who saw the rapid firing of people he himself had selected as a sign of strength rather than strong evidence of bad character judgment.

But not all those exiting the revolving door were incompetent. Some let it be known to their close friends that they could not stand working for a man who had no idea what it meant to be president of the United States. No administration in American history, at least in modern times, could match the chaos, confusion, and rancor of this one.

A sense of potential doom was building, and predictably it arrived in the wake of an election defeat. Authoritarians do not like to be voted out of office, especially one for whom the ultimate condemnation is "loser."

Within minutes of the announced outcome in states the president assumed without question would vote for him, allegations of voter fraud and ballot counting manipulation filled the airwaves from the White House.

In retrospect, it now seems inevitable that the events of January 6, 2021, were bound to happen. Options were few, certainly within the Constitution, so the manufactured insurrection against the Capitol of the United States was as inevitable as a Shakespearian tragedy.

And it was that. To see the House and Senate chambers desecrated by barbarians was heartbreaking. This was the cathedral of democracy. In the twelve years I was fortunate enough to represent the people of Colorado in the Senate, not a day went by that I did not catch my breath when entering the chamber.

If ever American democracy is lost, the turning point will be January 6, 2021.

Mr. Trump still has with him close advisors whose publicly stated goal is to dismantle the government of the United States. That is actionably treasonous in itself. Little more evidence is required to know that the drums you hear are the drums of authoritarianism on the march.

The American Republic created by our Founders almost two and a half centuries ago is in jeopardy, sooner rather than later. Should it die, it will be the result of a network of violent extremist militias on the one hand and the lassitude of the American people on the other.

At stake are the sovereignty of the people ("a Republic, if you can keep it"), the commonwealth of America, resistance to corruption, and the banner of civic duty and honor.

It would be comforting to believe that the infamy of January 6 was a historic aberration never to be repeated. There is no assurance of that. Those who instigated that unprecedented insurrection are still walking around, free men and women. And they are laying plans for the 2022 and 2024 national elections that will virtually guarantee their success.

Mr. Trump has a clever practice. It is to condemn his opponents for actions he has taken or is planning to take. It is fiendishly clever and the ultimate distraction from actions he is planning. The Big Lie, that the 2020 election was stolen by fraud, is now the justification for erecting systems in crucial states that will actually be fraudulent and guarantee his desired outcome in those states.

But first, the rule of law must be set aside, quietly if not blatantly. Partisan court packing is the most obvious sign of this. Judges whose beliefs, inclinations, and persuasions are right of center are a crucial element. Partisan ownership of the Department of Justice and its affiliated offices throughout the country is also crucial. Recruitment of police and military officers and troops for right-wing militias is underway as well, although estimates of success vary. Subversion of progressive and liberal political campaigns is reportedly on the rise.

Hand in glove for authoritarians with subverting the people's law firm, the US Department of

Justice, was stacking the federal judicial system from district and appeals courts up to and including the Supreme Court itself, the entire third branch of constitutional government.

The US Fifth Circuit Court of Appeals in New Orleans upheld the state of Texas's ban on abortions, reversing a very recent district court decision overturning that ban on constitutional grounds. That decision was left standing by the Supreme Court. However one feels about the issue of abortion rights, this is but one of a mounting number of higher court rulings supporting one wing of the Republican Party.

Politics of one kind or another has always played a greater or lesser role in federal judicial appointments. But in modern times there has rarely been a period when the appointment of judges and the decisions rendered by those judges hewed so closely to conservative doctrine.

Which raises an even more thorny question: Are the most conservative elements of the Republican Party tilting toward some brand of Trumpian authoritarianism? For the good of the nation, one would hope the answer to this question to be no. But few deny that a new kind of fear factor is at work among the few remaining "moderate" Republicans and more traditional conservatives.

Without public attribution almost all political reporters have talked with Republican members of Congress who attest to the fact that many of their colleagues acquiesce to Trump's wishes or refuse to contradict him for fear of attacks from his "base." This, even though a preponderance of the insurrectionists of January 6 were from that base. Party over nation, and cult over party.

A word must be said about the transition of the Republican Party from traditional conservatism to its current authoritarian model, a Trumpocracy. I served in the Senate with a number of principled moderate Republicans who could legitimately trace their heritage back to Abraham Lincoln. I also served with a number of principled conservatives such as Barry Goldwater, Mr. Conservative himself, and we became friends.

Several deviations thereafter laid the groundwork for the cult of Trump to hijack traditional Republicanism. It is notable the number of well-known Republicans who claim their ideological heritage but go out of their way to separate themselves from the political party the cult has created. A number of us, including leading Democrats, wish for the return of traditional conservatism and believe in a two-party system.

But aberration is not limited to the sharp right turn of parts of the Republican Party. Lifelong Democrats abhor new trends of "cancel culture" and the rise of an illiberal left within the Democratic Party. Those trends find no roots in the Party of Franklin Roosevelt through modern-day Democratic presidents.

Thus, while deploring the real dangers of authoritarians and insurrectionists, Democrats must be wary of ideological excesses within their own midst. Both traditional parties must find constant occasions to root their ideologies in the principles of the Declaration of Independence and the Constitution as well as the lives and histories of our great leaders since our founding.

It is yet another strong reason for the restoration of civic education in our public as well as our private school systems. Young people need to know, especially in this age of upheaval and distraction, who we are as a people and a culture. That kind of education will hold a mirror up to the fearful excesses of insurrection and return us to our historic foundations.

C.
Tribal Nation

The authoritarian tendency divides and conquers. The United States is becoming disunited in several ways. American citizens increasingly see themselves as members of a tribe. The tribe may be regional, familial, social, political, professional, religious, racial, gender based, or a mix of a number of these.

Human beings have formed social groups virtually throughout history. People sort themselves out and seek communication with those sharing common characteristics. We are naturally comfortable with people like us. We sense common beliefs, interests, and experiences and bond with those who share similar characteristics.

Nothing concerning here, except . . . except when loyalty to the tribe, especially politically, replaces loyalty to the nation. Then, the tribe comes first even when it is at the expense of the nation and its interests.

Not a thing wrong with garden, book, poker, or sports clubs. Concern arises, however, when a group sees itself outside the nation or the nation's interests threatening to its own identity. That is when tribalism replaces national identity and cohesion.

Then, the nation, usually identified by its government, is seen as a threat to or enemy of the tribe. Frictions arise. Threats are imagined. Identity, then security, are threatened. And gun sales rise.

Some years back, in 1998 to be exact, I wrote a book called *The Minuteman*. It traced the history of militias in America from their appearance in the Second Amendment to the Constitution to the present era. Originally, the Founders saw them as domestic protection against foreign aggression. They resisted the notion of a standing professional army in peacetime.

Now, as we have visibly seen, not least on January 6, a significant number of militias have arisen, and experts increasingly express concern about their threat, especially among the more secretive militias, to our domestic national security.

This concern may be directed at a more vivid form of tribalism, but it is also a heavily armed one.

We have a large network of professional law enforcement agencies, chartered under state and city laws. We also have in each state a national guard organized by statute to serve the purposes of the Second Amendment mandate to protect the homeland. Until it is federalized, rarely, the state national guard is commanded by duly elected governors of the respective states.

So, what specific purpose do heavily armed, often secret, private militias serve? A main theme in their public and certainly in their private utterances is resentment of their own national government, the government of the United States.

If for no other reason than their availability to authoritarian movements, this separate armed tribalism is a matter of concern during a time characterized by insurrection against our nation's government. This is sufficiently obvious as to require no further elucidation.

So, during the most recent Trump years (future ones may follow) we have seen the tentacles of authoritarianism reaching into the Department of Defense ("my generals"), the Department of Justice (perceived as the president's personal law firm), the courts and judicial system up to and including the Supreme Court, state election offices and personnel appointments, voter suppression laws and bizarre voting audits with no evidence of fraud, and now armed secret militias organized around antigovernment agendas and publicly willing to mount insurrections.

But this all happened *after* gaining control of the Republican Party. That was the necessary first step. And that control continues to this day. If you question this assertion, ask Elizabeth Cheney.

Further spread of the authoritarian tendency may be documented too late. That tendency is here, has taken deep roots, and gives evidence of undermining our democracy already.

Should this continue, it bears repeating at length, not only will democracy become a wistful memory, but the American Republic, willed to us by our Founders, will exist no longer.

Authoritarians find the idea of popular sovereignty anathema to their longing for one or another kind of dictatorship. They do not concur that there is anything like a commonwealth of common good and common interest. They systematize corruption, placing personal over national interest. They explicitly reject the ancient republican concept of civic duty, engagement, and participation.

Even today, the pillars of the American Republic, whose flag we salute, are being undermined.

The emergence of cultural and political tribalism in our nation is welcomed by the neo-authoritarians.

It is easier to overthrow a democracy and its national values and norms if that democracy is fracturing into tribes, and identity is with one's tribe and not our nation.

The goal of authoritarianism is the replacement of American democracy and the Republic upon which it is founded with a single executive surrounded by a Praetorian Guard in the White House, a cabinet of loyal disciples, and a party in Congress that does as it is told.

This looks pretty familiar.

D.
Press and Media
in the Authoritarian State

Throughout this essay, I frequently refer to the Trump-led political movement as a cult rather than a political party. Except for the elected and party officials it has suborned, it has little resemblance to the traditional Republican Party, yet it carries its banners as if that is what it is.

The Trump movement has no manifesto, no platform, no set of shared beliefs, no substantive identity, no set of qualities its adherents share. It is a perfect vehicle for an antidemocratic cult. Whatever you believe, you can join so long as you show up for the next insurrection.

Any common themes are negative. Burn it down. Shred the government. Attack the system.

The central theme is: power. We demand power. We want control. We will run things. We don't want your votes. We demand your loyalty.

Traditional Republicanism throughout most of the twentieth century, if not before, was characterized by fiscal conservatism, balanced budgets, smaller, much less powerful government, and, certainly after the end of World War II mid-century, by an interventionist foreign policy bolstered by an ever-expanding military presence worldwide.

Some of that still lingers, but the Trump movement is neo-isolationist, suspicious of international relations, willing to cut taxes severely even with no spending cuts, and reckless on its management of the national government.

So, the new authoritarian movement, characterized most vividly by its January 6 insurrection against the US government and its Constitution, is something never seen before and maintains its connections with the traditional Republican Party only through intimidation, a characteristic of authoritarian regimes throughout time.

Among the first things that occur in the transition of a democracy to authoritarian rule is the demand from the state that media outlets perform according to the state's diktat and publish and promote the interests of the authoritarian rulers.

In a postdemocratic American era, that exercise of powers would seem unnecessary. There are dozens of print publications, periodicals and newspapers, that already promote daily the Trumpian cult. And, most notably, Fox News, OANN, the Sinclair network, and other electronic outlets routinely provide favorable coverage to those interests willingly.

Rather than creating a media support base on command, however, the Trumpian cult inherited one looking for a leader. The media outlets mentioned, and they are far-flung, required little instruction from the Trump White House press office. Indeed, the operation often worked the other way: right-wing press and media set the Trump agenda, and policies followed their instructions.

In office as well as since, the relationship of the neo-authoritarian cult to its media advocates is symbiotic: tell us what you are going to say today, says one to the other, and we will say the same things. An authoritarian takeover, therefore, would require little if any media takeover because the supportive media base is already there and willing to perform.

This is not to say that a full-scale authoritarian takeover would deal lightly with the much-derided "mainstream media"; the *New York Times*, established television networks, traditional centered cable news programs will all continue to be pilloried and marginalized. As we know today, Trumpian followers listen religiously to Fox News to get the marching orders of the day and no other outlets that do not tell them what they wish to hear.

E.
Systems on the Brink

Uncertainty and confusion are the enemies of democracy. Democracy flourishes in stable times. Authoritarian appeal grows when conventional and traditional systems become or even seem to become fragile and faltering. Leadership by command and fiat are believed to be needed to stem the tide of collapse.

Even stable, strongly rooted people begin to worry when an airline unexpectedly cancels all its flights, throwing entire air travel systems into disarray. Bitcoin and cryptocurrencies seem to destabilize money and banking. Computer network hackers, including ransomware hijackers, take down whole communications systems. Every day, citizens are harangued by robot callers getting their credit card and social security data by trickery. Many citizens don't know whom to trust and are drawn to certainty, and certainty is the coin of the authoritarian realm.

Mussolini made the trains run on time.

Nothing has contributed more to uncertainty than the Covid-19 pandemic. Seven hundred thousand Americans have died and tens of millions more worldwide. Hospitals and care centers across the nation have operated at or near collapse. Experienced nurses and health-care workers have come down with the trauma condition known as PTSD out of exhaustion both physical and mental.

For more than two years traditional lifestyles have been disrupted. Office workers do not go to offices anymore. Commuters stay home. The very nature of work itself is undergoing a revolution. If office workers can work at home, who needs expensive office space? Great buildings are idle and empty. The entertainment industry, theaters, concert halls, and restaurants have been badly disrupted.

Although most of this has to do with economic disruption, social and political disruptions have occurred also. The political world now revolves around masks and vaccines. The stark national divide has less to do with liberal versus conservative confrontations and much more to do with trust in science.

Cynics note that some of the most ardent opponents of masks and vaccines are Republicans who have surreptitiously gotten their shots and worn a mask to get into a favorite restaurant but equally ardently publicly rant against both.

But the psychological and social damage of the pandemic is by far the worst price. Even Mr. Trump and some close to him experienced the virus. Those who have most vociferously flaunted their contempt for science have succumbed. The grim reaper sought them out.

The tide of authoritarianism is born up by increasingly fragile social and economic systems, and the continuing viral pandemic and will continue to rise as the search for certainty rises in a chaotic time.

Its fuel is fear that stagnates into anger.

F.
Obedience versus Duties

"We were sent here by the president," a number of insurrectionists said.

Democrats obey the law. Authoritarians obey the leader. And they are very willing to break the law, if the leader so instructs, in order to achieve power. Witness January 6.

This is the reason there can be no authoritarian approach to democracy and no compatibility of democracy with authoritarianism. It is simply a matter of obedience.

It is a central question for the House of Representative's Commission on January 6, the degree to which the insurrectionists felt they were carrying out Donald Trump's orders. Many stated that "we were sent here by the president."

If that is true, it is treasonous.

This is the point at which being a nation of laws, not of men, is crucial. Military forces obey the lawful orders of their commanders not merely because of their authority but because the orders are lawful.

The question becomes this: If an authoritarian president were to be elected in 2024 by the substitution of electoral slates chosen by legislatures out of obedience to that candidate as opposed to the popular vote, which will, of course, be alleged to be "fraudulent," what is the response of the courts but also the people?

Here, we must restore the core principle of the republic: popular sovereignty. Nowhere is the sovereignty of the people more manifest than in the vote. The people, not state legislatures, select presidential electors by their votes. This is why we are a Republic. And the specific instance of where our Republic can save our democracy.

Experts believe this is where we are headed in 2024. This issue will be raised in as many as sixteen states, but most crucially in three states that will probably decide the outcome: Pennsylvania, Wisconsin, and Michigan.

A political coup mounted by a presidential candidate, even one who is a former president, is nevertheless a coup, an overthrow of government, in this case the US government, by force. The force already underway for 2024 is replacing the sovereign people's vote by partisan state legislators selecting their own electoral slates regardless of the popular vote.

An argument was made by insurrection supporters that those conducting the assault on the Capitol were merely "exercising free speech."

Every law student in the first semester of the first-year class on Constitutional Law (always shorthanded as "Con Law") learns that the First Amendment guarantee of freedom of speech is not absolute. And the illustration is graphic enough to be remembered: you cannot shout "fire" in a crowded theater.

On several occasions the Supreme Court has sought to define limits on speech, perhaps most recently in the *Brandenburg vs. Ohio* case where it ruled: advocacy could be punished only "where such advocacy is directed to inciting or producing imminent lawless action and is likely to incite or produce such action."

It is a matter for discussion and debate whether provocative remarks by President Trump at the rally before the assault on the Capitol was advocacy inciting lawless action.

Apparently, few if any of the insurrectionists on January 6 who launched themselves as barbarians inside the gate had gone to law school. Pretty obviously they had not, or they wouldn't have been there committing several kinds and levels of criminal violations.

After serving their respective sentences, they may think twice before answering the summons to a second insurrection.

Yet, the insurrectionists' misguided supporters, including some members of Congress and party officials, repeat the mantra that these everyday American citizens and patriots, out of deep concern for a stolen or fraudulent election, as notable speakers at their precriminal march on the Capitol told them, were merely exercising their First Amendment guarantee of freedom of speech.

There are other restrictions on freedom of speech. Advocacy of violence is not contemplated. Yet, on the horrifying tapes of that infamous day, insurrectionists outside and inside the Capitol are heard to say, "Kill Pence," "Kill Pelosi," and other such patriotic slogans.

It is difficult to know which is worse, the barbaric insurrectionist assault itself or the high hypocrisy of its political defenders trying to minimize the massive offense and practicing the Trumpian high art of deflection.

Either way, the assault is now ironclad and copper riveted in future US history books for future young Americans to see and learn how close we came not just to insurrection itself but to successful insurrection and destruction of American democracy.

We must pray, and do much more than that, to prove wrong the present-day Prophet Jeremiahs who are warning that January 6 was a dress rehearsal for the ones to come in 2024. Perhaps if the defeated candidate continues to pursue a rerun of the 2020 election, he will hopefully so preoccupy himself with the past that he will be unprepared for the next trial.

Mr. Trump is a master of irony. He accuses his opponents of doing what he himself is planning to do, in this case stealing the election. His cult simply says, "The other side did it the last time so it's our turn now."

All that is required to carry this out is complete contempt for democracy, its standards, and its norms. But Mr. Trump has never shown any concern for any of this. He could not write a 500-word essay on democracy, unless the essay ended by him winning.

Autocrats and authoritarians think democracy is for weaklings. That despite the hundreds of thousands of members of the military services who have sacrificed their lives for our democracy over the decades. But, of course, those pesky bone spurs prevented any current would-be autocrats from sharing that experience.

Authoritarians may have their obedient cults. Most Americans prefer our two-and-a-half-century democratic Republic guaranteed by strong men and women who did their duty. America's patriots are the true winners.

G.
Democracy Is Strong

For two and a half centuries, democracy has survived and strengthened in America. This essay, devoted to saving democracy, in no way suggests it is weak. But announced plans, carried out in daylight, to replace the popular vote with decisions by partisan state legislators, supported by partisan election officials in those states, is arguably the most direct political attack on democracy and the rule of law in our nation's history.

This scheme alone warrants high alert on the part of democracy's defenders and those elements of the press and media concerned for their own constitutional protections.

If democracy has a centerpiece, a fulcrum, it is the integrity of the vote. The authoritarian scheme to use claims of fraud, while dealing fraudulently, destroys that centerpiece and directly attacks the heartbeat of democracy.

Were this scheme to succeed, all other aspects of democracy would be in immediate jeopardy. Fundamental rights and freedoms can be set aside or abandoned by authoritarians in power. Elections themselves can be delayed or set aside. Constitutional guarantees of freedom of speech, assembly, and religious worship can be, as in most authoritarian dictatorships, suspended.

This cannot happen, some will say, because our Founders created a system of checks and balances. The executive branch, the legislature, and the judiciary keep each other in check. Concentration of power in the executive branch will be offset by the legislature and/or the judiciary.

Having taken over the Republican Party, however, the authoritarians have successfully tilted the Supreme Court and many of the district courts and courts of appeals in their direction. In this term of the Supreme Court, voting rights cases may be the bellwether of whether the court is a balance to or complicit in authoritarian politics.

And, most directly, the lockstep of Republicans in Congress to support virtually every pronouncement of Mr. Trump and even to deny that the right-wing assault on our Capitol was urged and supported by him ("I will be there with you") demonstrates the intimidating power of the cult. For its members, the insurrectionist assault on our Capitol was merely a typical visit by peace-loving American constituents.

If the popular vote in some red and purple states can be set aside in favor of partisan electors in a presidential contest, so too can it be manipulated to elect partisan candidates for Congress and statewide offices.

Once again, the argument of fraud in voting as a means to fraudulently manipulate the outcome of the vote is laden with irony.

Based on the performance of certain courts and Republican legislators in recent years, it is problematic to say the least that the constitutional construct of checks and balances will save our democracy from authoritarianism.

Until the elections of 2022 and 2024 are freely and fairly conducted and the popular vote remains unmanipulated, all Americans who believe in democracy and keeping our Republic must remain on high alert and exercise vigilance.

The best protection of democracy is the bright spotlight of public attention. An authoritarian coup can only be successful in the dark. That spotlight should be turned on immediately . . . and kept on . . . throughout the next two election cycles.

This is not a fair fight. Defenders of democracy believe in rules and laws, civic behavior, and civilized norms. Unbound by these guardrails, authoritarians will stop at nothing. If proof is needed, merely look again at the videos from January 6. You will see mob behavior, destruction of the temple of democracy, and the search for high public officials to kill.

As some have already characterized it, this was a dress rehearsal.

Those who believe in keeping our Republic and defending the democracy it guarantees must mount the parapets on the walls of American democracy, maintain the spotlight of public attention, and hold back the barbarians of authoritarianism.

The price of failure is unacceptable. Future generations depend on us in the coming perilous time to keep our Republic in sacred trust for them.

H.
The Consequences of the Big Lie

The battle between democracy and authoritarianism in the next two national elections is over selection of presidential electors but also over voter suppression and control of the election process at the state and local levels.

A number of states, especially where the presidential vote was reasonably close, have been subjected to Trumpian demands for recounts and expensive audits. These are characteristically distractions meant to keep the issue of alleged fraud alive for as many months as possible.

Meanwhile, legislatures in Republican controlled states have been busy restricting access to voting aimed at minorities, young people, and others believed to be dependable Democratic voters. These voter suppression steps include restriction or elimination of mail-in ballots, reduction of voting places in Democratic precincts guaranteeing long waiting times in line, reduction or elimination of drop boxes, prohibitions against making water available to those in waiting lines, and slow processing of voting, among many other restrictive practices.

A strong movement is underway in many of these same states to place conservative Republicans in key election offices at state and local levels. As election expert Mark Elias has written: "Voting rules that maximize participation result in fewer disputed outcomes, while complex and restrictive rules create a larger pool of disputed ballots that can be used to justify post-election challenges" ("How the GOP Will Try to Subvert Our Elections," *Democracy Docket*, October 13, 2021).

The net result of this election maze is to guarantee fewer voters, especially among those assumed to be Democratic voters, through complex voter suppression measures, to place Trump-aligned election workers in key local and state positions, and to guarantee enough confusion to justify postelection audits if necessary to reverse results.

The social and political fallout from the spreading of the Big Lie is distrust in elections generally and particularly those who are authoritarian cult supporters.

This dagger is aimed directly at the heart of democracy. Trust in the integrity of democratic elections is central to trust in democracy itself.

The pattern has become very clear. Mr. Trump will reject any election he does not win. This is a classic definition of authoritarianism. But even if it is called something else, it cannot be called democracy.

I.
Anatomy of a Coup

Americans have no experience with a coup attempt to overthrow our government. We had Civil War, but that involved one part of the country declaring itself separate from the other part of the country openly and notoriously.

A coup is the overthrow of our government from within largely by surreptitious means. It is civil war on the sly.

The coup-plotter-in-chief, Mr. Trump, actually began the coup during his 2016 national campaign. He did so by taking the obligatory first step, casting doubt on the traditional media. The "mainstream media" he proclaimed are not to be trusted. They promote "fake news" and should be disregarded. Don't believe what they write and say, was the message. This was easy for early cult followers, he knew, because they already got information, more likely propaganda, from Fox News and other sources who told them what they wanted to hear and already believed. It was in its way a perfect positive feedback loop.

Mr. Trump and his merry band of pranksters already had a ready-made propaganda machine. Most authoritarians have to create their own news networks or take over state-owned media.

Then skip to the fall of 2020 when national polls were reporting either a close race or a Trump defeat. Machinery was put in place to begin to undermine the integrity of the election if Trump were not reelected. The only fair elections are those he wins.

When states such as Arizona and Georgia, which he assumed would vote for him because of adherence to traditional Republican patterns were declared against him, the coup broke into the open. The president himself called state election officials, many of whom were Republicans, and requested or demanded that a few extra thousands of votes be "found" to reverse the outcome.

When a candidate's principal epithet is "loser," we all should have known what to expect.

When network returns showed Senator Joe Biden to be the president-elect, the coup began in earnest. Election integrity is at the heart of democracy. It not only had to be questioned, it had to be shredded. And shredded it has been since election night.

The farce of a recount in Arizona is well known. Despite its failure to reverse that state's outcome, demands for recounts, almost always in urban areas, were demanded in Georgia and Texas, which Trump won, and northern states, such as Pennsylvania, Wisconsin, and Michigan, as well.

This was a clever pattern. The Trump cult could try to reverse the 2020 outcome, which Trump himself has never given up on, while casting doubts about the integrity of elections in key states for 2024 at the same time.

As background to this drumbeat, any success by the Biden administration had to be undermined as well. The tragic partisan divide became a chasm. With a few notable exceptions, such as the handful of Republican members of Congress who voted for the second Trump impeachment, Republican minorities in both the House and the Senate have opposed in lockstep virtually all Biden administration initiatives. A one-vote Democratic margin in the Senate, because the vice president is president of the Senate and can break a tie, has been rendered useless because of the filibuster.

So, Republicans whose states and districts would benefit from large-scale infrastructure measures, for example, nevertheless opposed them by cutting off their noses to spite their faces.

Two key measures of a coup: question the integrity of democratic elections and derail programs of the administration in power to undercut its credibility.

A third step is to create one's own reality. Nowhere has this been more evident than in the case of the January 6 insurrection. The murderous and bloody attack by the Trump cult, at the behest of Mr. Trump and his cohorts, against law enforcement authorities, was described by Republican members of Congress as simply ordinary citizens come to visit the Capitol as on any other day.

Their motto seemed to be: Who are you going to believe, me or your lying eyes?

It is left for each of us to decide whether a treacherous event of this magnitude could have come from the Democratic Party. And this insurrection was not mounted by the traditional Republican Party, but by the Trump cult. The moral tragedy is the early denunciation of the event by some Republican leaders only to reverse course under threats from the cult.

Sometimes a party requires too much, John Kennedy once said. But the threats against defectors from Trump came from the cult and not the traditional Republican Party. The Trump cult now holds the Republican Party hostage. The ransom demand is return of Mr. Trump to the White House.

That would, of course, be the triumph of the coup and the insurrection. Republican majorities in the House and Senate and a conservative majority in the Supreme Court eliminate any chance of "checks and balances" so trusted by America's Founders.

Return of Mr. Trump to the White House in 2024 through election manipulation, partisan state legislatures replacing the popular vote, and partisan election officials selected for that purpose amounts to the culmination of a successful coup, the overthrow of our government by surreptitious means.

Even more profoundly, that also would be the end of democracy in America and the hollowing out of the American Republic.

This threat should cause all American citizens to think deeply and seriously about our country. Who are we now? Have we become a different nation and society in the last few years? Do we really still believe what we used to declare that we believed?

Such a national exercise in introspection might be necessary for us to reclaim our birthright, to truly become American patriots once again. Elections are not simply about selecting leaders. They are also a canvass of our beliefs at that time. Canvass in the polling sense, but also canvas in the artistic sense . . . a picture of America and the American people.

The cult's attack on democracy and the sanctity of our votes is the most serious threat to our nation's security since the insurrection of the Civil War. But, as mentioned, this threat is not open and direct. It is internal and insidious. It is a cancer that spreads in the dead of night and with little notice.

If this coup fails, as it must if enough honest, decent, law-abiding, patriotic Americans rise up, decades from now books will be written analyzing how this all happened. It is a new experience for us. We were not trained or educated to anticipate this devious set of circumstances. They are outside the American character and our nation's history.

If we survive this unprecedented experience, as we must, we might see a genuine restoration of our Republic and with it our sense of citizen duties. That itself would be the best bulwark against the next wave of coup-plotting barbarians.

Bring back civic education to our schools. Raise voter participation well above 80 percent of eligible voters, as opposed to our current 60 percent or less. Make our flag ubiquitous and not the possession of one political party or another. Genuinely honor our military volunteers and care for those who are wounded or old. Celebrate our nation's birthday not just with fireworks and parades but also with town meetings and services of prayer and thanks.

The challenge is not merely to defeat this coup attempt but also to make that victory the occasion for national renewal, social cohesion, and restoration of and respect for our highest and best national values.

J.
The American Republic and Elections

Most republics throughout history have elected leaders through the exercise of the sovereignty of the people. Leaders of republics have understood that they worked with and in most cases for the people as citizens of the republic. The history of republics demonstrates that failed republics almost always resulted from leaders elected by the people assuming power over the people and thus becoming dictators.

The twenty-first-century American authoritarian cult believes itself to represent the people.

But it will not accept the judgment of the people in a free and fair national election. There is little if any evidence that the cult members, particularly in its insurrectionist wing, understand the sovereignty of the people as demonstrated by election results.

Likewise, we find no evidence that the cult and its leader have any understanding whatsoever of the meaning of a commonwealth, the common good belonging to and owned by the people themselves. Mr. Trump and his White House seemed to believe that everything managed by our national government belonged to him and his family.

Books by and with the assistance of Trump insiders are replete with instances of noblesse oblige, that it was all there for the taking. By contrast, former president Harry Truman was asked in interviews with Merle Miller (*Plain Speaking*, Berkeley Publishing Corp., 1973), what mementoes he took from the White House. Truman said, "Nothing." Miller pressed: surely there were a few pencils, notepads, desk items. Truman said, "I took nothing." Miller was stunned. "Why not?" he asked. Truman said, "Because none of it belonged to me."

By contrast, gifts from foreign leaders, expensive bottles of whiskey, and a variety of other items of value have gone missing after the Trump years, even though the law required them to be archived. So much for the commonwealth, and a decent respect for the nation of laws.

As for resistance to corruption required by republican doctrine, the record speaks for itself whether special interests or the common good and national interest should prevail. Trump properties here and abroad became the obligatory accommodations for Secret Service, traveling military units, cabinet officers, and US government employees, and in Washington, for visiting foreign leaders and their parties. Except for the latter, all at US taxpayers' expense.

And, on the checklist of qualities of republics, including the American Republic, is civic duty, the obligations of citizenship required to protect the rights of our democracy. The continuing theme of the 2020 election, still being contested with no evidence, was manufactured votes ("Find me 12,000 votes in Georgia"). The theme emerging well in advance of 2024 is voter suppression and overriding the popular vote.

All of this violates the principles of republicanism and the American Republic. Far from the argument here that adherence to those principles can save our democracy, the plan underway from the Trump cult for 2024 could destroy our democracy and the Republic of our Founders at the same time.

K.
The American Republic, Its Preservation

Our immediate concern here is the prevention of treachery by authoritarianism in America's democracy. That threat is real and historically immediate. It can plausibly be argued, separately, that the nature of this threat has never been faced by American government in our history.

That is why the qualities of our Republic offer the best shield against this threat and, perhaps, why our Founders were more brilliant than even they realized in using the concepts and language of the historical republic to create our new nation.

Even in those early days, however, enlightened Americans had enough knowledge of democracy to insist, over the objections especially of Adams and Hamilton that we were also a democracy. As one would expect, it was left to Thomas Jefferson, as pointed out earlier, to correctly say that we were in the process of becoming a *democratic republic*.

Therefore, while the authoritarian threat confronts us in ever more vivid terms with ever more frightening consequences, several decades from now scholars and everyday enlightened American citizens may conclude that in protecting our democracy from authoritarianism we also, intentionally or not, redeemed and restored our Republic.

In a profound study of republics and republicanism entitled *The Machiavellian Moment*, the scholar J. G. A. Pocock described how Machiavelli revived the ancient ideal of republicanism and sought to apply its principles to a world, in this case the Principality of Florence, at the dawn of the Renaissance in Italy and the predawn of the English and Scottish Enlightenments.

These days if we think of Machiavelli at all, we think of the manipulative author of *The Prince* and his cunning thoughts on the uses of power by the Medici. But he was much more than that and in the fifteenth century virtually singlehandedly resurrected the idea of a republic as a form of governance, one that might reconcile an emerging new world of commerce, governance, and learning eager to shed the chains of medieval times and open up new ideas and thoughts that would become the Enlightenment that so influenced our Founders.

Given our immediate—and they are immediate—concerns with neo-authoritarianism in democratic America, further exploration of Machiavelli's role is a detour. But, to reiterate, what our challenge may involve is not simply the protection of American democracy against a mindless authoritarian cult, by resort to our Republic and its ideals. It might also, indirectly, result in bringing the American Republic of our Founders to new life, by dusting it off and showing its relevance to the dramatically changing age in which we live.

That would be a bonus, and a valuable one. Therefore, keep in mind that in using republican ideals to protect democracy from authoritarianism we may also be introducing a renaissance of republicanism in the coming times.

First things first, however. Keep in mind we are proposing to employ popular sovereignty, the sense of a commonwealth, resistance to corruption, and civic duty to protect our democratic rights and freedoms. This effort to reconcile republicanism and democracy and send them into battle against the forces of authoritarianism will require new categories of thought among opinion leaders, elected officials, the media, and commentators across the ideological spectrum to embrace unfamiliar ideas and language they are largely unaccustomed to.

It is a subtle approach to render a blunt instrument ineffective by changing the nature of the debate. The authoritarian cult minimizes its reduction of democracy to slogans and stage sets. It will find it more difficult to convince truly patriotic Americans to stop saluting our flag "and the *Republic* for which it stands."

L.
Power, for
What Purpose?

Power, in the political sense, is amoral. That is to say, it can be used for good or for ill. One of the major purposes of political campaigns is for the candidate to answer one question: What do you want to achieve?

The Party of Trump has no manifesto, no platform, no agenda, no statement of purpose or goals. It is simply to give Donald Trump power.

To do what? We have bits and pieces of a jigsaw puzzle of what he is against: Democrats; international agreements; ObamaCare; climate action; taxes, for sure; the media, except those that flatter him; regulations; state dinners; allied states people; most public lands and resources; military troops who get killed or wounded; and a number of other things he dislikes.

What he is for is less clear. He has a curious interest in dictators; rally crowds; long, rambling speeches; Fox News; personal attention; tax cuts; and then it becomes distressing to try to find ideas, issues, policies that might interest him.

He covets the limelight, so long as it is flattering, but not the responsibilities of governing. He seems remarkably incurious about most things.

But he does single-mindedly want power. Once again, the question recurs: To do what? An adherent might say, to stop the many things he does not like. That is power as veto.

As to concrete Democratic programs and policies on a wide range of matters, he is against them without even saying why. This is best described as dog-in-the-manger politics: I don't want to accomplish anything, and I don't want anyone else to do so either.

Any student unlucky enough to be assigned a term paper on Trump's governing philosophy would stall after an introductory hundred words.

That he is such a blank page philosophically and practically has its advantages. His cult members can fill in the blanks as they wish. He can be all things to all people simply by closing himself off in the TV room.

I had breakfast with Mr. Trump when he was up-and-coming in New York City real estate and seeking to find a niche. He had called my Senate office and asked to get together on my next trip to New York. This would have been sometime when I was preparing for a second national campaign, probably in 1987.

I felt he should know more about what I thought and how I saw national leadership in that era and provided bite-sized policy statements to pique his interest if not also his engagement. But my recollection is that this did not get very far. He did offer, without my request, to raise money for the campaign in New York City and Mar-a-Lago, which I believe he had just purchased. At that point I believe there were some polls already showing that I was leading other candidates, including prominent Republicans, by comfortable margins.

In any case, the occasion did not arise and we never met again, although I did invite him to stop by my Senate office if he got to Washington. He was pleasant, outgoing, seemingly relaxed and convivial. Given all that has happened since, I've thought about the encounter often and wished that I had been given the opportunity to know him better.

It did cause me to wonder whether the fund-raising offer was a way of positioning himself for a high-level position in a new administration. We will never know. In any case, he ended up getting the highest-level position more or less on his own.

Mr. Trump served one term as president and appears to be preparing to seek another, that is if he is not "reinstated" as president by proving he was fraudulently denied victory in 2020.

In either case, should he succeed, the question will still arise: For what? Having little sense of or interest in history, perhaps he does not know for what? The big White House is still there. There would be Secret Service for protection. Republicans in Congress would eagerly do what he told them. And he might even be fortunate enough, God willing, for the virus to have gone away.

A recurring poetry line from high school is: "Breathes there a man with soul so dead that never to himself has said, This is my own, my native land."

It is not for me, or I suppose anyone else, to render judgment on the soul of another human being. And, if for no other reason than that he seems to care for and promote his children, he possesses a soul of some kind. But what does he think about his native land, his America. He gives lip-service to some kind of patriotism but limits his respect for those military veterans who don't get captured or killed. And he lowers the flag at the death of only those who support him.

Candidates for the presidency should be required to write an essay of some length on why they wish to be president and how they feel about our country. Why do you want this power and what do you intend to do with it?

That would be more awkward for some than for others.

M.
Barbarians,
Inside the Gates

The transition of republics to autocracies, authoritarianism, dictatorships, or tyrannies is often accompanied by civil unrest, and the suppression of that unrest is the reason given for concentrated empowerment in the hands of the few or the one that is tolerated or even demanded.

There was some of this in the transition of ancient Rome from republic to imperial power. There are occasions throughout history, most recently perhaps in the so-called Arab Spring a few years ago, when popular forces seeking democracy and freedom overthrew autocrats and dictators with ultimately mixed results. Those featured more mass public protests than actual assaults.

The wonder of the January 6 insurrection is that America saw it come and go and then moved on. Or did we? There are still some 600 criminals to be tried and sentenced, so the issue will occupy at least page six in most papers. Thereafter, feature stories will pop up about what this or that insurrectionist who participated in cop killing is doing today.

The ostensible purpose of the insurrection was to suspend the constitutional process for selection of a president by overruling the popular vote and thus crush the heart of our democracy.

Lest we become so desensitized that we can witness and forget anything, however mean and destructive, this incident has to make its way into American history textbooks so that future generations can learn how close we came to the destruction of our government and possibly even the assassination of a vice president, speaker of the house, and other members of Congress. They need to know how it happened and who was responsible, up to and including the president of the United States.

The assessment of responsibility is now the task of the House Select Committee on the January 6 Insurrection. Republicans, including some who rightly were appalled and aghast, are now hoping it will all go away and be quickly forgotten.

It cannot be forgotten. Americans attacking their own government had never happened before. The British burned the White House in 1812 and we did have a bloody Civil War of secession. But nothing like January 6, truly a day that will live in infamy.

As someone for whom the United States Senate chamber was my office for twelve years, I saw the barbarian destruction of that chamber and the rest of the Capitol and wept. It was worse than a bad movie. The barbarians sitting at the desk that I occupied or one very near it rifled through the private papers of senators, demeaned the desk of the presiding officer, and purportedly took the occasion to perform further vulgar acts.

The US Capitol is the temple of democracy, not just for America but also for those large parts of the world that long for our system of government . . . or at least used to. Aside from searching for officials to kill, while contributing to the deaths of several law enforcement officers (remember the "party of law and order"?), what did these barbarians think they were doing?

Supposedly most of them thought that, at the president's behest, they were interfering with the constitutionally mandated counting of electoral ballots reflecting the popular vote outcomes of a number of states. They failed, because after the Capitol was finally cleared with belatedly arriving law enforcement, the House and Senate reconvened and carried out their responsibilities. All the rest of it was pure destructive theater to please the emperor watching on television far from the violence (despite the promise that "I will be there with you").

Are there lessons to be learned from this tragic assault on democracy? Most certainly. For the vigilant, there is already the warning from senior military leaders that January 6 could well have been, in their words, a "dress rehearsal." The heavily armed right-wing militias, a number of whom participated in the insurrection, are still intact and available. There are more than enough leading Trump followers available and willing to resume the rhetorical insurrection at least.

And the prevailing theme of the Big Lie, that the 2020 election was stolen, is there to inspire, as false as it is. So, there are the pieces for the main event: armed troops, firebrand inspirers, lessons learned from the dress rehearsal, and the Big Lie.

Any hope that the Big Lie would simply run its course has proven false. There is plenty of evidence from fascist risings in Germany and Italy in the 1930s to prove how durable false themes can be for those who want to believe them. While we deliberate, as we must, as to why true believers choose to believe false themes and Big Lies, we must also expect recurrence of the "dress rehearsal" on a larger stage.

We still have the 2022 elections mere months from now and the second act of the 2020 psychodrama two years thereafter. Plans are well underway in key states to steal those elections on the grounds of preventing them from being stolen. You can't make this up.

The threat of violence is always in the wings. So, those of us not in the inner security circles in Washington must hope and pray that the Pentagon, national guards, state and local police forces, and intelligence agencies are on the alert and planning for virtually any eventuality. We do not need to expand our domestic security structures. We do need for them to be much better prepared with working scenarios and training for another and possibly larger January 6.

If anything can happen in the world of insurrection, with the cast of characters still at large, it probably will. Concerned citizens do not need to be afraid, but we do need to be highly alert.

Until we find ways to bring our nation back together, and particularly to break down the bitter partisan divide that plagues us and our government, we will still have tribalism and identity politics to deal with. Unlike the threats faced by the United States almost throughout the twentieth century from fascism and communism, today our worst threat is here at home. It comes from neighbors who look and act just like us. They are being told that we are trying to steal their government from them.

If members of Congress and appointed officials fear for their and their families' safety, democracy surely will not survive. Even simply the presence and threat of violence causes us to trade freedom for security. This very condition is the threat of insurrection.

Our national challenge for at least the next three years and possibly beyond is to contain and then eliminate the continuing threat of insurrection, internal violence against our own government and our democracy.

But we must use democratic means to do so. The worst possible outcome would be for the forces of democracy to believe they must adopt violence to counter violence. That is a prescription for civil war. Then we have not only lost our democracy and our Republic but we will have become another country.

V.

THE FUTURE OF
OUR DEMOCRATIC REPUBLIC

A.
Concluding Thoughts

We must save democracy in America. Restoring our Republic is the approach advocated here. It is the most positive way to achieve both objectives: saving democracy and bringing back the republican principles and ideals in which our Founders believed and which they felt were critical to the survival and flourishing of the United States.

Because an increasing number of experienced and dedicated patriots are issuing warnings against creeping authoritarianism, warnings dramatically increased after the January 6 insurrection, there is now a guardrail being erected against apocalyptic warnings that frighten concerned citizens into lassitude and inaction.

There is a fair amount of alerting contained in this essay, if for no other reason than to wake up those who haven't been paying much attention. That slumber is, in large part, the result of assurances by forces to the right of traditional conservatism that January 6 was just a walk in the park and nothing to concern ourselves about.

The price of liberty, and democracy, is eternal vigilance. My effort in this essay is to waken that vigilance and provide a positive and constructive way to push the authoritarian tendency back into the basement where, even so, it will continue to brood so long as there are those looking for the proverbial man on a white horse who will take control and ease our fears. That man will only ask that we give him the authority and power he seeks, but at the cost of our freedom.

Resisting apocalyptic warnings is difficult once one becomes aware that the authoritarians are not operating on the margins of our politics but are instead aiming a quiver of arrows at the heart of our democracy . . . the ballot box.

The crucial first step in obtaining power is to limit the vote, in this case of the elderly, the young, and minorities. This increases the power of the votes of those who are more likely to welcome in the authoritarians who sing their song.

Elections are a measure of who we Americans are by asking us who we would like to manage our government. They are central to democracy and, in that respect, must be treated with secular sacredness. Every indication to date causes us to think about 2022 and 2024 as particularly important given the latent and actual insurrections in the wings.

Other serious and experienced patriots will continue to increase the drumbeat of warning as those dates approach. It is my purpose here not only to join that drumbeat but even more importantly to provide a positive and constructive way out of a dangerous political cul-de-sac.

Well before the 2020 elections, I joined several former senior government officials in forming Keep Our Republic, a group dedicated to protecting the core of democracy, the vote. Two of its members, Mark Medish and Jonathan Winer, are proposing a Compact for public officials and everyday concerned citizens. Here are the words of the proposed Compact:

> *We Americans are blessed with a reliable, free and fair electoral system that works to ensure that the voices of the people are*

heard. For generations, our elections have been safely and soundly implemented by officials and volunteers at the state, county, and precinct levels. We cherish these civic traditions which have made our country the beacon of democracy around the world. We rededicate ourselves now to uphold the following basic principles, and we call upon our fellow citizens to do the same:

    Let every eligible voter vote.

    Let every vote be counted.

    Let the electoral count stand.

    Respect the voice of the people in each state as expressed in the popular vote.

The sovereign American people, by remembering our commonwealth and resisting the corruption of authoritarianism, and most importantly by exercising our civic duty by voting, are invited to join us in this Compact that will help save American democracy.

To achieve these objectives, we must push back strongly against voter suppression, efforts to minimize voter turnout, and partisan control of the election process itself. Despite the Big Lie, it has been proved over and over again that fraudulent voting is practically nonexistent. But the authoritarian-in-chief and those close to him will continue to promote the Big Lie daily to cast doubt on the election processes so long as they fear defeat and the hated word "loser." For them, once again, the only legitimate elections are the ones they win.

At least through the next presidential election in 2024, and perhaps beyond, we all must be prepared to strengthen and broaden the vote and access to the ballot box. Simply because voter suppression and partisan control of elections may not be happening in our state does not mean that these practices in other states will not turn out electoral votes for president regardless of the popular vote outcome.

The singular purpose of this twofold evil, voter suppression and partisan election control, is to take control of and reverse election outcomes that do not support authoritarian candidates. It is massive *real* voter fraud operating behind the smokescreen of *alleged* voter fraud.

Various steps to control the outcome of national elections are not occurring in every state.

We are dealing with efforts in so-called red states, and states such as Pennsylvania, Wisconsin, and Michigan, whose electoral votes in 2024 will probably determine the next presidency.

There are several prescriptive plans to open, rather than close, voting doors. Almost all call for transparency in voting access and counting. Election officials should be nonpartisan or bipartisan, not representatives of one party alone. The ballot and the ballot box should by readily accessible to all.

At stake in democratic elections is trust. Every effort on the far right is to spread distrust, to forecast fraud even before election day, and to question any unfavorable outcomes. This is a sinister dagger aimed at the heart of American democracy. It is a cynical effort to drive a wedge between the American people and their government.

The struggle of the last few years, continuing onward, is between two visions for America. One is an attempt to turn back the clock to a time when white males ruled, borders were sealed, trade was curtailed, and America reverted to an era before it assumed global leadership of democracy. The other vision is continued American political, security, and environmental leadership globally; a fair, bipartisan immigration policy; social and racial justice; and resistance to international hegemony without seeking hegemony.

Every effort to return to a perceived, but often imagined, better time is doomed to fail for the simple reason that times change and realities change and democratic policies must change with them to remain relevant. Policies must adapt to new realities, but principles and ideals should never change.

And our current struggle is to protect and preserve America's best principles and ideals.

We take American democracy for granted at our peril. That is why our Founders stressed so strongly the republican concept of civic duty (in their words, civic virtue). We have a Republic "so long as we can keep it." And keeping it involves, at the very least, voting in every election, national and local, and paying attention to what is at issue in that vote, while resisting strongly efforts to nullify our votes.

B.
A Democratic Republic

There are common characteristics of democracies throughout history and in different parts of the world, although there are distinguishing differences on the margins of each. The same is true of republics throughout the past two and a half millennia, although they share certain characteristics that make them republics.

And our Founders made it clear at all points in their deliberations that they were applying the republican formula to the government of the American continent stretching out before them. Virtually to a person, our Founders believed and so said and wrote that they were forming the Republic of the United States of America.

As discussed earlier, to this day there is remaining confusion as to how we describe ourselves, and most Americans find it easier to say we are a democracy than to say we are a Republic. Also, confronted with confusion early on, Thomas Jefferson settled it by saying we are a *democratic republic.*

Adopting the Jefferson formula, and following rules of language, "democratic" is an adjective modifying the noun "republic." Thus, the American Republic adopted over time democratic political rules and values.

But our republican foundation possesses the qualities repeated in several contexts here that may protect our democracy from real and perceived threats against it, beginning at the heart of all democracies, the ballot box. If we Americans do our civic duties, including especially protecting access to voting and dismissing false charges of fraud, as sovereign citizens we will also protect our commonwealth and resist corruption.

We are a Republic that practices democratic principles and processes, in a word.

For those wishing to revitalize the ideal of the American Republic of our Founders, especially as a bulwark against recent antidemocratic trends, the recommendations throughout this essay are available. These include:

★ Restoration of civic education in our school systems that teaches the duties of citizenship;

★ Encouragement of citizen participation in all levels of government, including local government boards, town hall meetings, candidate and elected officials' forums, school board and community hearings, and a wide variety of citizen gatherings;

★ Insistence on the ideal of popular sovereignty and the accountability and responsibility of elected and appointed public officials to the people;

★ Citizen self-education on the breadth and scope of the commonwealth, all those resources and assets that belong to all the people;

★ Participation in a variety of nonprofit organizations that seek to close the revolving door between public service and lobbying;

★ The exercise of civic virtue, or civic duty, by participation, engagement, and involvement in the proper functioning of all levels of government;

★ Finding outlets of speech and press that are committed to facts, science, and truth in educating the public on government activities important to all the people, not simply as sources of ideological certainty.

Although I chose, rather late in life, to return to the academy and write a thesis on republics, I make no claim to scholarship and was much more a political practitioner, at least for a brief period. I have always been more a public servant than a politician.

If this essay should fall into the hands of serious scholars who wish to challenge either my treatment of republics or discussions of a democracy in peril, their thoughts are more than welcome. Nothing is more therapeutic than a reasonable and honest debate.

Our purposes here are merely to explore the nature of the American Republic as a source of guidance for dealing with latter-day challenges to our democracy and to offer not just resistance to those challenges but to provide a positive and hopefully creative path forward.

Were my plea for a resumption of the study of civics in our public and perhaps even private schools to receive any attention, a discussion of the sort sought to be provided by this brief essay might be a starting point.

Likewise, though not pleasant, a serious discussion about the dangers to our democracy of the unprecedented January 6 insurrection should involve every member of future generations as a warning as to how a destabilizing pattern of such incidents could bring our great nation to its knees.

To keep our Republic and protect our democracy every effort must be made to expand, not contract, access to the ballot box. If the states now passing laws and regulations making voting difficult, and administering those laws and regulations by partisans carrying out the authoritarian wishes, that process can spread beyond red and marginal states to the nation at large.

Authoritarianism is a cancer. It will corrupt the democratic host upon which it grows.

It is tempting for me as a former officeholder, elected twice in Colorado, to promote my state as an election model. We have open access to voting, with absentee and mail-in ballots that are sent to voters' homes, drop boxes are readily available, and our elections are conducted on a bipartisan, nonpartisan basis by skilled election workers and votes are counted accordingly. With only very rare exceptions, challenges to voters or ballots are rare indeed.

States like Colorado are the rule, not the exception. The effort now to control elections on a partisan basis in a dozen and a half states is narrowing democratic rights and freedoms to a dangerous extent, and there is no valid argument for it.

As an American with considerable experience in and around government in our nation in a wide variety of capacities, I know our country's foundation to be strong, principled, decent, and fundamentally democratic. We must keep it that way and resist any temptation to tamper with that democratic foundation.

That requires widespread citizen attention and engagement on a continuing basis but especially at election time. In a busy and complex world at this time, there is always a temptation to let someone else worry about it.

During this period and for a few years to come, that will not work. Our national slogan must be, "All hands on deck." We owe that to ourselves. But we owe it more to our children and future generations for whom we hold our country and its ideals in sacred trust, and we owe it as well to our forefathers and -mothers back to our founding, and we owe this duty to all those generations who have sacrificed their lives to keep us free.

I have been an idealist all my life and very late in life remain one where our country is concerned. At some cost, I have no doubt we will triumph over our current antidemocratic threats and challenges. It is for each of us to make the pledge to do so.

By being vigilant and doing our duty, we will save our democracy and restore the American Republic.

★★★

This essay is a plea to save our democracy by restoring our Republic and halting the covert but head-long rush toward an authoritarian state.

This proposal is straightforward: restore and revitalize our democracy by restoration of the principles of our Republic.

Gary Hart

United States Senator (Ret.)

(D.Phil., Oxford. Thesis:

Restoration of the Republic [2001])

SUGGESTED
READING

Bailyn, Bernard, *The Ideological Origins of the American Revolution*. Cambridge, MA: Harvard University Press, 1967.

Banning, Lance, *The Jeffersonian Persuasion: Evolution of a Party Ideology*. Ithaca, NY: Cornell University Press, 1978.

Bock, Gisela, Quentin Skinner, and Maurizio Viroli, eds., *Machiavelli and Republicanism*. Cambridge, UK: Cambridge University Press, 1990.

Dagger, Richard, *Civic Virtues: Rights, Citizenship, and Republican Liberalism*. New York: Oxford University Press, 1997.

Fischer, David Hackett, *Albion's Seed: Four British Folkways in America*. New York: Oxford University Press, 1989.

Hamilton, Alexander, James Madison, and John Jay, *The Federalist: A Commentary on the Constitution of the United States*. New York: Modern Library, 2001.

Hart, Gary, *The Minuteman: Returning to an Army of the People*. New York: Free Press, 1998.

Hart, Gary, *The Republic of Conscience*. New York: Blue Rider Press, 2015.

Hart, Gary, *Restoration of the Republic: The Jeffersonian Ideal in 21st-Century America*. New York: Oxford University Press, 2002.

Machiavelli, Niccolò, *Discourses on Livy*, trans. by Harvey C. Mansfield and Nathan Tarcov. Chicago: University of Chicago Press, 1998.

Machiavelli, Niccolò, *The Prince*, trans. by Tim Parks. New York: Penguin Books, 2009.

McCoy, Drew R., *The Elusive Republic: Political Economy in Jeffersonian America*. Durham: University of North Carolina Press, 1980.

Montesquieu, Charles de, *The Spirit of Laws*, ed. by Anne M. Cohler, Basia C. Miller, and Harold S. Stone. Cambridge: UK, 1989.

Pocock, J. G. A., *The Machiavellian Moment: Florentine Political Thought and the Atlantic Republican Tradition*. Princeton, NJ: Princeton University Press, 2016.

Richard, Carl J., *The Founders and the Classics: Greece, Rome, and the American Enlightenment*. Cambridge, MA: Harvard University Press, 1995.

Rousseau, Jean-Jacques, *Of the Social Contract and Other Writings*. London: Penguin Classics, 2012.

Sandel, Michael, *Democracy's Discontents: America in Search of a Public Philosophy*. Cambridge, MA: Harvard University Press, 1996.

Skinner, Quentin, *Liberty Before Liberalism*. New York: Cambridge University Press, 1998.

Taylor, Charles, *Philosophical Arguments*. Cambridge, MA: Harvard University Press, 1995.

Tocqueville, Alexis de, Democracy in America, trans. and ed. by Harvey C. Mansfield and Delba Winthrop. Chicago: University of Chicago Press, 2002.

Viroli, Maurizio, *Republicanism*. New York: Farrar, Straus and Giroux, 1999.

Wood, Gordon S., *Empire of Liberty*. New York: Oxford University Press, 2009.